THE

Gay Uncle's

GUIDE TO

Parenting

CANDID COUNSEL

FROM THE DEPTHS OF THE

DAYCARE TRENCHES

THE

Gay Uncle's

GUIDE TO

Parenting

Brett Berk, M.S. Ed.

THREE RIVERS PRESS

NEW YORK

Disclaimer: In the interest of full disclosure (and to protect me from the wrath of my friends and family), I want you to know up front that the stories in this book are not all one hundred percent true. Most of them are what I like to call tru*ish*, reflecting things that actually happened, but with some liberties taken—melding bits and pieces of different events or people or exaggerating painful situations and details. All of this has been done primarily to protect the innocent—or the guilty. But, because I'm not averse to cheap shots, it's also sometimes done just to get a laugh or simply to make me look smarter. In every case, the objective is to make a point, and to make it in a way that bursts your bubble and pokes you in the ribs. If you're planning to read this book, I hope you like that feeling.

Library of Congress Cataloging-in-Publication Data
Berk, Brett.
  The gay uncle's guide to parenting: candid counsel from the depths of the daycare trenches / Brett Berk.—1st ed.
  1. Child rearing.   2. Parenting.   I. Title.
  HQ769.B5186 2008
  649'.1—dc22   2007020604

ISBN 978-0-307-38138-5

Printed in the United States of America

DESIGN BY ELINA D. NUDELMAN

10 9 8 7 6 5 4 3 2 1

First Edition

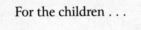

For the children . . .

Contents

Contents

THE
Gay Uncle's
GUIDE TO
Parenting

Parenting as Pinball

WHENEVER MY THREE siblings or I complain to our mother about some heinous practice she employed in our childhood, something that could loosely fall under the rubric of "parenting"—forgetting to pick us up from Hebrew School; staying out until 1 a.m., riding the mechanical bull; simultaneously driving and whacking at whichever of us she could reach with a plastic spoon she kept in the glove box—her retort is always the same: "You kids didn't come out with an instruction manual stapled to your foreheads."

Some pop-psychologizing would suggest that perhaps I got into working with young kids as a way of correcting for having grown up in a "broken" home. There may be some truth in this. It's certainly true that after my parents divorced, they both quickly abandoned the wee Berk four: Dad married a born-again Christian and renounced us; Mom worked twelve-hour days in sales and trolled the singles bars at night. It's also true that this arrangement left my younger sister and me with the task of raising our little brother, switching off caring for him like two teenage parents (albeit ones who never spoke).

It's also possible that I fell into the world of early childhood through an accident of economics. I was the only boy in the local babysitting pool, a fact that made me appealing to our neighborhood's growing cohort of divorced moms, all of whom wanted their kids to have some sort of male role model. Though I was hardly ideal as a dad substitute—I hated sports, I couldn't grill—I routinely made twenty-five cents an hour more than the girls. And being the only male applicant was an advantage that carried over when I finished college and started looking for paid work as a teacher. (The rate of pay remained unchanged as well.)

But after more than twenty years as an early childhood educator, I've come to realize that I gathered all of this knowledge so that I could write the elusive book my mother was always talking about. (Note: do not staple this to your child's head.)

This book is not for parents who want to raise a perfect child. You can probably make that kind of kid, but I don't think you should. I've met more than my share of young prodigies—kids who were pushed to skip grades, memorize the Latin names for every insect, and greet all adults with firm handshakes. They're weird, and not in a good way, like a corgi wearing a tuxedo: sure it's cute, but does it truly know joy? This book is for people who are tired of feeling pressured to have that kind of kid, who are fed up with having to hear about, or act on, every parenting trend that comes down the pike. This is a book for those of you who want to be parents as well as people, who don't want to feel guilty about taking some time for yourself or your relationship (if you're even in one). It's for those folks who might, every once in a while, want to get drunk, and have sloppy sex without worrying that they're going to roll over on their kid because you all sleep in a "family bed" since that's how they do it in Taiwan and they have the highest math scores of any country on earth. This book is for parents whose gut instinct is telling them that it's probably not any healthier or "cooler"—for anyone involved—for them to be their child's best friend than it is to be their merciless overlord. This book is for parents who want to find a way to return a sense of balance to their life, and to the lives of their kids.

Wait, you say. There's already plenty of information out there on this topic. In your most recent perusal of the parenting section on Amazon, you've seen a number of titles to this effect: *Why Breast-Feeding Is Worthless, How to Unprogram Your Fetus, Why You Should Put Your Kids in Foster Care RIGHT THIS MINUTE* and *Go Back to Being the Big Drunken Slut You Once Were.* Well, I'm going to let you in on a little secret: those books are all flawed. Why? Because they're all written by parents.

Now, I have to give parents their props. An incredible ego release is required in order to smother a child with the kind of blind unconditional love that is necessary to perform the job properly. In fact, it was seeing firsthand—as a preschool teacher—just how difficult parenting is that convinced me that I was not cut out for it. But blind unconditional love, by definition, must contain some blind spots. My job in this book is to shine a light onto these. A bright light. A klieg light, actually. So, consider yourself warned. I'm going to be snide. I'm going to poke fun. I'm going to call you out on all sorts of crap you didn't think anyone had noticed. But you have to remember, I'm not doing this to be cruel—or at least not *only* to be cruel. I'm doing it because I love kids. (News flash: people don't work in preschools for the money.) I'm charmed by their humanity. I'm in awe of the way they piece together information. And I've dedicated my entire adult life to creating means to help them succeed. But by not being overly invested in their every move, by not needing them to like me all the time, and by having attempted and borne witness to a wide range of profoundly unsuccessful strategies, I've developed a unique perspective on how to raise them: I'm an outside expert.

You might counter that much of my position is predicated on my ability to divest and even, at times, to walk away. You might say, *You* don't have to live with them. I would wholeheartedly—and thankfully—agree. But I would counter-counter that this doesn't inherently make my position any less valuable. (Not all dentists have cavities, and not all plastic surgeons have face-lifts.) In fact, it might actually enrich my perspective. Haven't you learned that distancing yourself from drama—especially family drama—can be an extremely useful tool? If not, perhaps you should meet my mother. (On second thought, maybe you should just try it on your own.) Moreover, there seems to be a national trend that favors entrusting the satisfaction of our most personal human needs to gay men. Americans have already ceded to us the right to clothe, style, groom, and feed them—and to good effect—so it seems logical that there should be room in the world of child rearing for the kind of bitchy yet benevolent role played by your hairdresser or interior decorator: someone fully invested in your needs but holding their own perspective; someone who can offhandedly throw together things you never imagined could be combined; and someone who can seduce you with highly functional concepts that you suspect won't work, but you actually find totally liberating. Voilà: *The Gay Uncle's Guide to Parenting (GUG).*

Using humorous anecdotes from my life with my family and friends, from my experience as a teacher and preschool director, and from my work as a consultant to some of the world's biggest producers of kids' media, food, and toys, this book will examine the dilemmas of modern parenthood and elucidate the job's most important rules. Funny little charts, checklists, and tables will supplement these tales, and help you learn how to zoom out of the PARENTING BUB-BLE, and see your life—and your kid—with fresh eyes.

"A PARENTING BUBBLE," I hear you say. "What the hell is that?" Well, I'm glad you asked, because it's a key feature of this book. A PARENTING BUBBLE is the external manifestation of a degenerative psychological condition, one that is brought on by living with a child full time and/or spending your time solely in the company of people who live with a child. The most common symptom is an inability to maintain perspective on your own actions. Those afflicted start to claim all sorts of crazy things: that primary colors are acceptable in decor, that Jell-O is "fun," that baby poop doesn't stink. If a case becomes profound, the infected may even ask their friends to *smell their baby's poop.*

A **PARENTING BUBBLE** is a dangerous place to be, not only because of the side effects described above, but because it impairs one's ability to make rational decisions. This grows from what organizational psychologists call groupthink. Groupthink is a faulty decision-making process in which the desire for unity and unanimity blinds people from considering or acting on functional alternatives, and it is precisely what allowed NASA to let the space shuttle blow up and the United States to enter into a disastrous and unfounded war in Iraq. When a dangerous situation like this comes up in this book, I will sound the alarm, and provide a **PARENTING BUBBLE ALERT!** These alerts are not only meant to wrench you out of groupthink—to literally burst you out of the **PARENTING BUBBLE**—but also to fill you in on the whys and hows of the situation, as well as instructing you on what you can do to fix it.

Fortunately for you (and your kids), escaping from the **PARENTING BUBBLE** is not as impossible a journey as repairing the space program, or resolving our troubles in the Middle East. It doesn't entail earning a Ph.D. in astrophysics, or the need to learn arcane dialects. It doesn't even call for body armor. But it does require you to recognize three major, and interrelated points:

1. Children are not simply little grown-ups.

2. Young kids see, understand, and react to the world *very differently* from adults.

3. Your children are not your equals; they're your dependents. (That means *they* depend on *you*.)

Think of it this way: young kids are like a ball in a pinball machine, zinging around from bumper to bumper seeking reactions. It's the job of the parent to show them the acceptable pathways and to deliver appropriate responses: to be the flipper, so to speak. If you flip carefully and expertly, you'll keep the ball in play and achieve a high score, and everyone will have a pretty good time (or as good a time as can be had playing pinball). If you don't react quickly or with proper modulation, the ball will plunge through the middle and spiral away until your next turn. And if you are indelicate, you'll get a tilt, and lose control of the flippers entirely, and the ball will just ricochet about madly on its own. Do you remember that asshole you knew in your youth, the one who always banged on the pinball machine, yelling at the ball for what was clearly his mistake? Do you remember how stupid that person looked? This book will help you *not* be that person.

By providing an outsider's perspective on some of the most fraught and desperate aspects of child rearing, this book will help you to shift the way you view your core job. It will help you to see that seemingly complex problems often have simple solutions. And it will allow you to envision child development not as a series of discrete emergencies that need to be immediately extinguished or resolved, but rather as one continuous (albeit nonlinear) process, of which you are distinctly at the helm.

Pretend You're the Grown-Up

How will I accomplish all this, I hear you asking. By demonstrating the value (over and over again) of a little role-playing game that you can try whenever you get stuck, one that can help you to remember perhaps the most important rule of raising kids: *the parent–child relationship is not one between equals.*

I first developed this little game early on in my teaching career, to help Anton, an adorable Estonian boy who was a student of mine during my first year in the classroom. I actually made it up to help Mika and Oskar, Anton's parents. They had come into my office one day with a dilemma: they were struggling with Anton's morning routine. Much to their chagrin, their son refused to eat his breakfast unless he was sitting under the kitchen table. With his stuffed turtle. And the cat. And a Dora video playing. And once he finished, he refused to come out and put on any of the myriad outfits they picked out for him or any of his many favorite pairs of shoes. And when they finally crawled under the table to get him dressed, he would lie stiff as a board, scream bloody murder, and refuse to cooperate.

"I just don't know what to do," his mother said, nearly crying.

I hadn't yet had much experience with hysterical parents, so I didn't provide much in the way of comfort or small talk. Instead, I just launched into an answer. I told Anton's parents that accomplishing the steps in a morning routine—like almost everything with young kids—is about balancing schedules, input, and choices, and that within this, there were a host of things about which Anton could have a say: he could pick from *two* preselected kinds of cereal, he could choose which seat he wanted *at the table,* he could decide which of *two* preselected shirts he wanted to wear. But Anton couldn't handle making *all* the morning's decisions. He wasn't capable, and he was spiraling out of control because he felt overwhelmed by all this choice and responsibility. He needed parameters. He needed limits. And he needed someone to lay these out for him. Anton's folks were exasperated with him for making their mornings chaotic, but I posited that if *they* took on the job

Weird Routines

We all have harmless bits in our daily routine that may seem silly or stupid when viewed from the outside: checking twice to make sure the oven is off before leaving the house, slathering pricey but useless creams on our faces to "prevent aging," blogging. Kids can have these tics as well: pointing out every fire truck that passes by, needing to test the bedroom light switch five times before bed, demanding Concord grape juice with their fish sticks when white obviously goes better with seafood. These kinds of routines empower them and help them feel that the world is a safe and stable place—a useful and comforting practice in light of the streams of new information they're constantly asked to take in. But when your child's oddball behaviors compound to become unmanageable or rigid—spending every waking minute in an old refrigerator box, changing their outfit eleven times before leaving the house, refusing to eat any food that isn't blue—it's likely that you're normalizing the unacceptable. These weird routines are usually a sign that something's gone wrong: that you're avoiding your responsibilities as the decision maker and/or paving over confrontation for short-term ease, and that your kid is reeling and looking for limits. It is your job to be in charge and provide a sense of guidance. Your child is not developmentally capable of such things. And even if they were, would you really trust their judgment? Look at how little their brainpan is. Do you really think they're as smart as you?

of being in charge, they might find it in their power to coax their befuddled little Hitler out of his bunker. I alerted them that they'd fallen into a **PARENTING BUBBLE.**

Mika and Oskar looked at me as if I didn't understand the depths of their dilemma. "We've already tried everything," they explained. "Everything."

I stared back, puzzled. *You can't be serious,* I thought. The problem was obvious: they'd given up the driver's seat and were treating Anton as if he was capable of taking the wheel. They couldn't see the way in which the control they were ceding to their son, instead of empowering him, was causing him strain. They couldn't see how they were driving themselves crazy by trying to cater to Anton's needs when he had no idea what these needs were or how to define them—because *he was three.* And they couldn't see how everyone's lives were being asked to collapse around this, like shrink-wrap, creating a hermetic world featuring their least attractive neuroses.

I sat up in my chair. "Let's do a little role-play," I said. *"Pretend you're the grown-up."*

Anton's parents looked at me like I'd asked them to solve Fermat's theorem. But after a moment, what I was suggesting sank in: I was asking them to imagine how their morning would run if *they were in charge, instead of their son.* The ensuing role-play was strangely useful, and I implemented it with some frequency after this: in parent–teacher conferences, in conversations with friends and family members, during fights I had with the slacker dad in the playground who stood by in silence as his evil spawn shoved the kids in my class off the slide. Though it was obvious, and more than a little patronizing, it helped usher parents toward the vital evolutionary principles that placed *them* in charge of their kids, and not vice versa.

To draw things out further, I would sometimes supplement the role-play with an accessible metaphor. The pinball one described earlier was very popular for a while, but as pinball itself receded beyond the range of parental childhood experience, I also developed one based on air travel. I would tell moms or dads to picture parenthood as an extremely long international plane ride in which their child is the passenger and they are the flight attendants. During such a trip, the cabin is the flight attendants' domain and federal law requires that passengers obey their instructions at all times. When the flight attendant turns the seat-belt light on, passengers are to be seated. When the flight attendant turns the seat-belt light off, passengers are free to move about the cabin. But there are constraints on this freedom. (Boundaries!) Passengers can go to the bathroom, they can chat animatedly among themselves, they can enjoy the use of preapproved electronic devices. But at no time does anyone get to play *outside* of the cabin or tamper with the lavatory smoke detectors or enter the cockpit and try their hand at flying the plane. And when the light goes back on and it's time for landing, there's no stalling or "Pretty please, one last chance." The rule is, sit down, turn off your iPod, and bring your seat back to the upright and locked position. Now we all know that there's nothing tremendously pleasant about a long international flight. But once you decide you want to go to New Zealand, there's really no choice about whether or not you have to get on board.

Of course, there are also times when, regardless of your years of in-flight training, other forces intervene and you are obliged to simply sit on the runway, caught in a passing storm system. This is what happened one New Year's during an overnight visit with our best friends Kate and Dylan and their eleven-month-old son, Max. It was the boy's first trip up to the country house I share with my boyfriend, Tal, and his parents' first time leaving the City with the kid, so we didn't want to impose too many rules or restrictions when they arrived. The result was a calamitous cold front of mayhem. The boy wreaked havoc on our homey cottage, knocking over anything that wasn't nailed down and shedding dirty diapers on every surface like an anaconda set to supermolt. He rejected the charming gift we gave him, a coffee-colored doll named Tanya who was exactly his size and wore an inexplicably slutty milkmaid costume. And he had a tantrum that ended only once he had kicked and beaten at his parents and worn himself to a frazzle in the center of our living room, where he sat naked, plunging his finger in and out of a puddle of applesauce, and watching an oddly Warholian video depicting nothing but the slab sides of a seemingly interminable freight train. "Train porn," our friend Dylan said, pointing blankly at the screen.

Standing there on New Year's Eve, watching my own house transformed into child-occupied territory, I felt horrified. I wanted to have nothing but positive feelings for my friends' kid. I wanted my friends to enjoy being parents. I wanted my house/life/peers back. But so many things had gone wrong during the visit that it was impossible to pinpoint any one useful solution or suggestion. I planned to talk this through with the assembled group over dinner. But Max totally lost it again during bathtime that evening, catalyzing a huge fight between Kate and Dylan, which ended in their barricading themselves in the guest room, and falling asleep before I'd even pulled the appetizers out of the oven. Tal and I ate dinner in near silence, brought a bottle of champagne upstairs, and watched a DVD on my laptop while drinking in bed. Tal's a huge fan of horror movies, and he'd picked George Romero's *Dawn of the Dead* as an appropriately apocalyptic film for the last day of the year. Leaning exhaustedly against the headboard, I tried to announce a clever correlation between the movie's mall-raiding zombies and the strange people who seemed to have taken over the bodies of our friends, but Tal just shook his head and shushed me.

"They're infected," he said. "They're doing the best they can."

1.

Sinking the Stockholm Syndrome

Going Out

OUR FRIEND ANGELA smirked guiltily as the waiter gave the cocktail shaker a final tremor. "I haven't done this in ages," she said.

Tal squinted in disbelief. "Had a martini?"

I squinted too. "Thought about your second martini before starting your first?"

"No." Angela picked up her glass with both hands. For someone who'd once been nicknamed Guzzles, she looked out of practice. "Gone out on the town."

"You call this 'on the town'?" Tal gestured at our surroundings. We were in a brand-new, brightly lit, sports bar/pool hall in a former warehouse in the middle of Helena—which, though it seemed to have only slightly more residents than our apartment building, is apparently the state capital of Montana.

Angela shrugged. "It's as close as they come around here."

"So then, this is your regular place? You come here and work the felts? Knock around the old stripes and solids?" Tal had had a pool table growing up, and in the rare circumstance in which we found ourselves around one, he took pleasure in tossing some lingo around.

"Sure. I've been here before. Of course. Though it's been a little while." Angela took another, slightly less cautious sip. "To be perfectly honest . . . it's been a long while." She nodded. "It's actually my first time here since Seymour was born." She sighed. "Truth be told, I guess it's the first time I've gone out at night *at all.*"

My jaw tried to drop, but I held it shut. Seymour was Angela's son—her nearly *three-year-old* son—the one successful product of her failed relationship with a failed musician, a drummer named Lawrence, who had pretty much abandoned her when she'd discovered she was pregnant. She had subsequently left Brooklyn and moved here, back home, to the allegedly warm embrace of her family. But while her parents assisted her financially—paying for Seymour's day care, and allowing her to work a low-paying job teaching English to female juvenile offenders—the limits of their support ended there.

I glanced at Tal. "I guess we sort of suspected as much."

Angela set her shoulders. "What do you mean?"

"Well, that twenty-minute monologue you delivered while we were waiting for our drinks? It was an annotated history of Seymour's recent bowel movements."

Ever the polite one, Tal perked up. "Not that it wasn't interesting. Really. I never knew that thing about the protective enzyme around corn kernels that keeps them from being processed by our digestive system."

"It would have been *more* interesting," I said, "if we weren't eating corn salsa."

Angela sighed. "Okay. I know. I should get out more. But it's so hard to motivate. I don't have any real friends here. I'm not dating—unless you count Lawrence dropping by for sex once a year when his band is in town. Plus, I miss Seymour during the days when I'm at work, and he's only up for a few hours once I get home. I want to spend it with him. I don't want to miss anything."

I nodded. "Fair enough."

"You don't mean that."

"You're right. What I meant to say was, you sound like you're suffering from a classic case of the Stockholm syndrome."

"How's that?"

"You know. When you fall in love with your captor . . ."

"I know what it is. But he's not my captor. He's my son. It's my job to take care of him—all the time. Plus he's just so cute . . ." She got a doelike look in her eyes. "I don't want to leave him, even for a second, especially at night, when he's so tired and sweet. We've developed our little evening routine, where I give him his dinner and his bath, and we talk about our days. Then we get into bed and I read to him and we snuggle. I curl up around him like he's a little stuffed animal, and . . ."

I cleared my throat, trying to break the spell of their insularity. I had seen this situation many times before: parents' unwillingness, or inability, to take time for themselves—to have a real adult life in addition to their role as a mom or dad. It came up in all kinds of families, from all manner of backgrounds, but it seemed to be more troubling for parents who felt isolated—physically, personally, emotionally—regardless of whether they were in a relationship or going it alone. Feeling stranded, their child becomes more central than they should, creating the potential for problems all around.

I moved my glass aside. "We need to revise your routine, before you become one of those bitter prairie spinsters—Willa Catheterized. Or worse, embarrass Seymour when he's a teenager by trying to accompany him to his prom. You need some You Time."

Angela hemmed and hawed, coming up with excuses as to why

she couldn't develop a social life. And though we tried rebutting her, she was tenacious.

"He's too young," she claimed.

"He's almost three. If this were the 1890s, or Malaysia, he'd have a full-time job by now."

"I have no sitters."

"Have you even looked? You can't be the only person in Helena with a kid. There are referral services, online postings, high-school bulletin boards. Or what about one of the young ladies you work with?"

"They're all criminals."

"Well, some of them are also mothers, right? Plus, isn't it part of your job to rehabilitate them?"

Angela looked down at the table. "Um . . . There's one other thing." She lowered her voice. "I'm sort of still breast-feeding . . . ?"

I clapped my hands together. "Now, we're getting somewhere." When pushed as to why a parent can't separate, I've found that this dirty little secret often emerges.

thanks for SHARING

One Tiny *GUG* Minute On: Kids' Personal Space

To parent well, you have to make your child a top priority. But being there for your kids doesn't necessarily mean being physically present *all the time*. For them to form a healthy sense of self—the idea that they exist as discrete individuals—young children need a balance between the security of your presence, and the space to explore where you end and *they* begin. This doesn't mean you should cut and run the day the cord is clipped. But safe, comfortable separation from you, and exposure to the new perspectives offered by other loving caregivers, can help provide your child with the templates and analytical skills—reaction, comparison, integration—they need for proper personal development. Having too close of a focus on your kids, particularly in the absence of other external outlets, also has the potential to create an unhealthy dynamic wherein your child's centrality in your life causes them to feel overly responsible for your well-being. This kind of responsibility is a grown-up's job. (And, remember, *you're* the grown-up.)

And as with most other practices about which we're embarrassed or defensive—watching soap operas, driving an SUV, obsessively checking our BlackBerrys—everyone has their own set of rationalizations

Breast-Feeding

I know that I'm not a woman, and I know that I'll never nurse, so I'm aware that making firm prescriptions about an age when I think children should stop breast-feeding (*by their second birthday, at the very latest*) will probably get me in trouble. I'm therefore going to skirt the issue as much as I can. (*Two boobs, two years max. Easy to remember.*) But please note that as with almost every other substantive parenting decision, *it's not your child's job to set limits. It is yours.* If someone found a way to put a tap in Tal's chest and make it run an endless river of icy-cold vodka or a foamy stream of berry smoothies with a protein blast, I know I wouldn't be the one to ask the pump to be shut off. However, I expect at some point, for both our sakes, that he would. Remember, they don't call it *weaning* for nothing.

as to why they can't stop. One of our friends claimed, without an iota of proof, that continuing to breast-feed gave her four-year-old son "social confidence." Another used the circular argument that she couldn't stop because her boobs got sore if she didn't let her three-and-a-half-year-old daughter nurse. Another said she let her five-year-old suckle only on special occasions, like at night—*every* night. Yet another said she was planning to stop but was waiting for her son to let on that *he* was ready. He could type at this point; I suggested he send her an e-mail.

I laid out my theories on breast-feeding for Angela, hoping she wouldn't go all La Leche League on me, but instead of agreeing or debating, her doelike gaze returned. "I just like the way he looks at me when he's nursing," she said. "It's like we're in love."

I tightened the cords in my neck. "Thanks for the honesty. But I think it's best if we all pretend you didn't just say that. The two of you will have to work that out later. In therapy." I folded my hands. "So, any other excuses why you can't leave the house?"

Angela thought for a moment. "Where would I go?"

"I don't know." Tal shrugged. "Out? Here?"

"Here? Why?"

"For fun?"

"You call this *fun*?" Angela sighed. "Anyway, who would I have this said *fun* with? Who would even want to have *fun* with me? I'm a thirty-six-year-old underemployed single mother. I'm overweight. I'm financially dependent on my family. And I apparently have nothing to talk about but the quality of my son's shit."

"If that's going to be your personal ad," Tal said, "I think we should probably do some revising."

Angela smiled but then squinted, almost looking like she was going to cry. "Do you ever get the feeling that you're playing a part—that you're acting out a role that's not the real you? I'm not sure if that's exactly what I'm feeling," she said. "But I left New York so suddenly, and I've been doing this mom thing so vehemently since, that I'm not certain who the real me is anymore. I know that I miss some parts of what my life used to be like. I miss playing the guitar at 2 a.m. after sex. I miss sex. I miss the guitar. The last time I even picked mine up was to pluck out a song from the *Finding Nemo* sound track. Try to tell me that's not enough to make me afraid to ever leave the house again."

Before she left Brooklyn, Angela had a great job teaching acting at an after-school program in the South Bronx, and a huge circle of super-funsy friends. But her true joy was performing in a lauded Heart cover band: Heart Attack. She had a tight wiry body, which she would throw around the stage with abandon, wailing and trilling, and the audience loved her because she was so obviously into what she did and not just one of those ironic hipsters for whom everything is an inside joke. She got a lot of play.

I could definitely see how she would miss her old life—especially since her decision to have a kid had not been something she'd planned but rather a scrambling reaction to an accident (read: mistake). But more than simply longing for her carefree past, her confession seemed to reflect two much more profound issues:

(1) she was feeling bad about herself, and (2) she didn't have an outlet for these feelings.

Just so you know, many, if not most, parents feel this way at some point. As a teacher, as a preschool director, even as the moderator of focus groups about kids' snack foods, I've had scores of parents tearfully confess their feelings of isolation to me for the simple reason that they feel they have *no other audience.* Parenthood can be a decidedly lonely place. People feel stuck inside their bubble, with no means, energy, or "justifiable" reason to escape. They feel as though they've lost touch with their former lives and aren't exactly certain about what they've become. And for all of the talk about the instant camaraderie extended by other parents, I've heard many more stories about people feeling excluded, derided, or misunderstood by their cohorts than I have about their being pulled into the warm embrace of parent-on-parent companionship.

This may be particularly true for the people I know, many of whom are, like me, total oddballs. But I imagine that it runs much deeper than this. Our friend Bridget says it's easy to find parents to talk to about superficial things—like her son's school schedule or his tantrums in the grocery store—but that when she tries to open up, saying things like "I kind of miss the occasional bump of cocaine," people tend to put their hands up in surrender and back away. She has taken to saying, about each new mother she meets, "That's another woman who's not going to be my new best parent friend."

I'm not suggesting that parenthood is solely a solitary slog. And I'm sure there are people out there who are entirely fulfilled by it and have no secret resentments or regrets whatsoever. I just haven't met these folks yet. What I often see around me are people, good people, who feel in some way stuck, scared, and/or cut off.

I'll say it over and over again in this book: we live in a country without a social support structure, especially when it comes to having and raising kids. Other countries have national prenatal programs to prepare parents for what to expect. Other countries have extensive family leave laws that help foster communication, cooperation, and partnership among families. Other countries have universal child-care initiatives to care for and educate parents and young children and to relieve some of the burden of trying to juggle work, home, and personal lives. Through a lack of foresight, a grotesque faith in "the market," and a blind mistrust of anything remotely resembling communism, we don't have any of these useful things. This leaves parents here with a dearth of resources. Perhaps more important, it also leaves them without a sense of community. Parents often feel like they have to do it all alone, and this places

thanks for **SHARING**

One Tiny GUG Minute On: Your Personal Space

While it is against the law in many states to leave a child under eleven alone, it is truly criminal for you to wait that long to take some time for yourself. There is no way that you can perform optimally at any job without breaks, let alone a job that runs 24/7 for your entire life. Being a parent shouldn't be seen as a selfless act of martyrdom any more than *not* having a child should be construed as selfish. It is a decision. And like any decision, you should be allowed to react to, resent, or regret it, so long as you don't do it too often (boring), with too much vehemence (dramatic), or in front of your kid (abusive). Taking time out from parenting—alone, with friends, with a partner—keeps you in touch with yourself. (Say it with me: "I am a parent *and* a person!") Without this outlet, you are likely to derive your notions of self-worth solely from your child. They can't, and shouldn't, be the only source to deliver this to you.

inordinate pressure on them: pressure that sometimes prevents them from realizing that in order to take care of their child and be an effective caregiver, they have to take care of themselves as well.

"You need to get out more," I said to Angela.

"No duh."

Angela sighed and seemed as though she was about to say more, to open up and avail herself to the idea that she deserved and needed breaks. But instead, she checked her watch, and acquired a panicked expression. "Shit," she said. "You guys have kept me out *way* too late. I have to go, right now, or tomorrow's going to be hell."

It was only 10 p.m., and the next day was a weekend. Even if Seymour got her up at 6 a.m., she could still get a decent night's sleep. But we'd had many of our parent friends act this way when we got them away from their kids: they feel guilty, they try to make us feel guilty, and they generally act as if we're all sneaking around, shirking responsibility by enjoying quality time with one another.

We gave Angela special dispensation because she was running the whole show on her own and had been since day one. But, in truth, our only parent friends who seemed immune to this tendency were the ones who were separated or divorced. Being a couple with a child seemed to create a wall of insularity for many of our friends, a cocoon that no one was allowed into, or out of. But once the first round of separations began, a magical freedom seemed to emerge, wherein our divorced friends with kids suddenly found themselves able to go out, and stay out, without remorse.

At first, this seemed based solely on custody arrangements: our friends could have fun on the nights their kids were sleeping at their exes'. But their behavior soon bled over into other occasions, and these folks became more likely to get sitters, set up sleepovers, or make child-care arrangements, even on the nights when *they* had custody. They became more fun, and found a more centered sense of self. Certainly there's nothing like a bad relationship to destroy your self-esteem and drive for amusement, but the change felt more comprehensive than this. It was almost as if, in disbanding their dysfunctional nuclear families, they'd been able to burst out of their **PARENTING BUBBLES** and liberate themselves from other restrictive structures in their lives, discovering that they didn't have to be slaves to their kid, they deserved to have some time to themselves, and didn't have to function solely as part of a conjoined whole.

This change clearly begged the question as to why all of this—sharing child-care duties, gaining perspective, being themselves—couldn't have happened before, back in the days when they were still in wedded bliss. My still-married friends Nila and Reese have long instituted a child-care policy wherein they switch off baby-sitting for their son Tomas: once a week, one of them stays in with him on their own, leaving the other one free to do as they please. Because it's structured, everyone knows what is expected of them. Because it's regular, they can plan in advance and don't have to make up excuses. And because it's based on reciprocity, trust and generosity are built in. They may not be able to go out together that often, but if they both want to see a particular movie, play, or exhibit, they each go on their free day and discuss it once they've both been. When I tell other couples about this, they seem to think it's revolutionary.

Of course, instead of waiting for, or mimicking, the liberating qualities of divorce, the easiest way to get out of the house is to hire a sitter. Yes, it's expensive. But even fifteen bucks an hour is much cheaper than the two hundred dollars an hour a shrink will charge to listen to you moan about feeling trapped, the three hundred dollars an hour you'll pay for a couples' counselor, or the four hundred dollars an hour a lawyer will bill to prepare your separation agreement. And yes, it can be hard to find one consistent person. That is why you need to develop a Sitter Stable. You don't have just one friend, or one pair of shoes, do you? No. Because proper support demands variety. (It's that whole eggs/basket thing.) Find two or three acceptable sitters, and use them on a rotating basis.

That way, you'll always feel like you have *options* instead of *an option*. Having options helps a person not feel stuck.

"Three sitters," you say. "Finding even one is so hard." I hear you. But let's be honest, this isn't like trying to locate an electable left-wing Democrat. This is finding a few decent, trustworthy human beings to watch your kid for a couple hours. Remember, setting an unattainable bar for who this person should be (Ph.D. in child development, your own doting but long-dead grandma) is only another self-defeating manifestation of the Stockholm syndrome. At my school, I hired a number of teachers who, on first glance, seemed questionable—a pink-haired male Cherokee performance artist; a brittle upper-class woman from Bombay; a formerly homeless African American lady with tangled dreads; a fast-talking, chain-smoking, aging punk chick—but who I could tell, from interviewing them and observing them with the kids, understood how to speak and be with young children and had an inner sense of balance, caring, and kindness. Think about your favorite babysitter from childhood. If you met her now, you might not hire her. But wouldn't you be making a mistake?

"I don't even know where to begin to look," I can hear you saying. But if you think about it, you've already got plenty of resources you can use to narrow your search. First off, you know other parents. (And don't lie to me and say you don't. I've seen you. You parents cluster together like clumps of seventh-grade girls.) You're not the only mom or dad in town who wants to leave the house once in a while. Ask some or all of these people for one quality babysitting referral. Second, since you were likely babysat for at least once in your life, think of who was hired to complete the task and try locating these types. If it's all too hazy, here's a list to jog your memory: neighbor kid, high-schooler, college student, nice old lady. If you can't access one of these folks on your own, someone you know probably knows, lives by, and/or has one in their family. Again, you just need to ask around. If you're too agoraphobic to make personal contact, or too busy to call, you can even use this great new invention I've heard of. It's called the Internet. If my friend Vernon can go online and find a man to have sex with within ten minutes of arriving in any town in the United States, with a little advance notice I'm willing to bet that you can use the Web to help find some candidates for your Sitter Stable.

I will demonstrate here by way of example. My sister Roxy and her daughter Amber recently came to visit us in New York, and since we wanted at least one night of grown-up dining—no interminable games of twenty questions at the table, no finishing the meal by 9 p.m., no limiting the number of drinks we consume—Tal and I decided to hire a sitter to come watch our niece. The hotel where they were staying had its own caregiver list, but that seemed suspect to me and didn't pass muster with Roxy, so I—someone who's never hired a sitter in his life—set out to deal with the situation on my own. I composed an e-mail listing the date, the number of hours, and the rate of pay and sent it out to about a half-dozen parent friends. They cc'd and forwarded it around for me, and within literally one hour, I had lined up two stellar sitters and had references on three or four more. Mind you, this was in the cutthroat atmosphere of Manhattan, where I've heard tell of people's unwillingness to even reveal their babysitter's name for fear of said sitter being stolen from under them.

Tal and I attempted one more push with Angela, trying to get her to stay with us a little longer—god knew when we would have some time together again. We even took the liberty of ordering her another drink. "We can discuss the formation of your Sitter Stable," I told her, quickly outlining the main points of my concept. I pointed

CHECK, PLEASE

YOUR HANDY GUG CHECKLIST FOR:
Finding a Sitter

A referral from a friend is a great start, but it's best to see a sitter in action before you hire them. Invite them over one evening for an hour while you're home, and have them do something fun with your kid like watch a video or eat pizza. (Note: offer to pay them for this time.) This will give you the chance to observe them with your child. It will also give your child an opportunity to meet and get used to them, absent the pressure of your departure. The kids in *Mary Poppins* had quite an exhaustive list of prerequisites (rosy cheeks, no warts, etc.). My checklist is much shorter. You should watch for the following:

❍ *Fun:* Hiring a stern old lady might make you feel more secure, but it's dreadful for the kids, and will eventually bite you in the ass. If you want to make this easy, pick baby-sitters who know how to have a good time. Remember, being responsible and being goofy are not mutually exclusive.

❍ *Forward:* That shy teenage girl might not complain when you stiff her on the tip, and she may always be available on Saturday night. But I've found that shy people often lack initiative with kids, especially if something goes wrong. Better to get someone who can speak up and take charge in a pinch.

❍ *Adequate:* Don't set too high a bar. You're never going to find someone perfect. But if you open your eyes, you're likely to find a stable of folks who'll suffice. Stop thinking that your every move is going to make or break your child's life. They're not made of glass.

❍ *Hot:* Okay, this one might be a little unfair to the kind, bearded auntie down the road, but think about how much more often you and/or your partner will want to go out if you hire a babysitter who's pleasant to look at. ("Why don't we have that nice girl Randi come watch the baby?") Note: don't flirt with or have sex with the sitter; that's *so* cliché.

❍ *Warm:* Children need to be hugged and held to feel secure. I'm much more freaked out by people who are cold and distant with kids than by those who are affectionate. I think it's the sneaky bastards you have to look out for, not the demonstrative ones.

❍ *Cool:* People who understand and get along with kids are able to roll with things, or steer them back, when life goes off plan. If a person looks tense all the time, they're probably not good sitter material.

at the martini. "By the time that's gone, you're going to have a means to solve your woes."

But Angela didn't want to hear it. Like so many parents, she seemed to find solace, or safety, in the idea that her situation was intractable. Through massive guilt, we managed to convince her to remain, but she kept looking at her watch.

"What's the rush anyway?" Tal asked. "Isn't Seymour with your parents?"

"Yeah," Angela sighed. But no sooner had she answered than she started in on what I like to call the Grandparent Gambit. This is the expectation that one's immediate family somehow owes them a certain amount of child-care service. "It's the first time they've sat for him in forever," she bemoaned. "I really thought they'd be much more forward in terms of helping out—giving me a break, doing their *job.*"

I smiled snidely. "I guess I haven't seen that job description. Exactly how many hours are grandparents supposed to put in each week?"

"Come on," Angela said. "You know what I mean."

I shrugged. This complaint is one I've heard many times before, but I disagree with it on a few different levels. First of all, your family didn't have the kid: you did. It's right to want them to be interested and involved in your child's life, but to do so effectively they have to be allowed to form a relationship that works for them too, not one that simply serves your needs. Second, I have learned that if you want something done right, it is best to remove it from the realm of obligation—particularly familial obligation—and turn it into a for-hire situation. Remember when you had your brother-in-law renovate your kitchen? Did that really work out better (faster, less aggravation, done the way you wanted) than hiring a professional? If you want a babysitter, hire a babysitter. If you want a grandpa, invite your dad over for dinner. Finally, the Grandparent Gambit is often a way of avoiding the real issue. If you can turn your situation into a familiar struggle—and by "familiar" I mean *known* as well as *familial*—then you can more easily mask the larger problem. By focusing on the idea that your folks aren't taking care of you (once again) you avoid the core dilemma, which is really about *you as a parent not taking care of yourself.*

Angela set up a time and place to meet us for brunch the next day, then left the bar in something of a huff. But since Tal and I had no other plans for our big night in Helena we decided to stay at Chicks with Sticks, and have some more drinks. After a quick survey of the people that populated the place—groups of secretaries gathering for girls' night out, overweight capital-city lobbyists in ill-fitting suits, and a smattering of hot laborers and college boys (what Angela called Local Talent)—the conversation returned to our friend and her predicament. We focused in on how strange it was that Angela had moved back home at all. She'd never been particularly effusive about her parents, often detailing how negligent they'd been of her in her childhood. It seemed odd that she would expect them to suddenly change and become warm and supportive. And it seemed stranger still that she would entrust them with caregiving duties. "Why do you think," Tal asked succinctly, "that the people who complain most bitterly about their parents' parenting are the ones who are so desperate to have them involved in raising their own kids?"

"A love of paradox?" I shrugged. "Gluttony for punishment?"

"I'm serious."

"So am I. Beyond what I've said, I'm sure I don't know."

"Then just trot out one of your tropes. You've never been shy about that before."

I put a finger to my temple mockingly but did my best to construct an answer. "In my experience, people often see having kids as a chance to correct the mistakes their parents made—to do things differently from how they were done to them. But if their actual parents are still around, I imagine that they can't help but gloss some of their own unmet childhood needs onto the situation. So . . . maybe they see it as a second chance to be taken care of properly?" I shrugged. "That would certainly make them desperate for their parents' attention. Which, when it's undelivered, would let them focus angrily on the fact that these needs remain unfulfilled, thus allowing them to feel vindicated by this disappointment and liberating them from having to analyze their own deeper emotions."

"Nice. But that seems like an unfair position to put your kid in."

"And yourself. And your folks."

Tal finished his drink and stared at a wiry thirties-ish guy bent over a nearby pool table. "Given all that," he said. "I really feel the need to help Angela out of her bind. And I like your idea about hiring hot sitters." He pointed. "What do you say we ask that gentleman over here for an interview?"

GUG'S TIPS FOR HANDLING:

Going Out

You are entitled to some time away from your child. This is not only appropriate, it is imperative for the maintenance of your sense of self and the smooth functioning of the parent–child relationship. Follow these instructions on your path to sanity.

- *On Your Mark:* Plan to go out right from the start. You're obviously going to be anxious about leaving when your kid is first born, but staying in for a few weeks quickly turns into a few months, and before you know it, your child's in high school and you haven't seen a single first-run movie that wasn't animated. The sooner you get out of the house, the easier it will be to make it a habit.

- *Get Set:* Begin lining up your Sitter Stable as early as possible. Introduce the sitters to your kid, and create a workable departure routine (story, hug, good-bye). Be sure to let your child know the steps in this routine *in advance*: contrary to popular belief, young kids don't like surprises.

- *Go!:* Head out. Day or night, weekday or weekend. It doesn't even matter what you do: go to a friend's place and take a bath; drive to the drugstore and buy some stretch-mark cream; sit in a parking lot and make phone calls if you want. The goal here is to create a pattern where you feel like you're entitled to some time away and a structure that allows you to feel comfortable leaving.

- *Keep Going:* Pick a regular date (every other Thursday) or a regular time (once a month for dinner) to leave the house. Routinization makes it easier for your child to deal, and it has the added benefit of helping you stick to the plan. Post it on your calendar, but again be sure to cc your kid.

- *Don't Look Back:* Your child might cry when you leave; they love you and like having you around. You're allowed to let this affect you; you love them and you're not a robot. But if you cancel your plans when-ever they cry, you're endowing them with authority beyond their capa-bilities. Remember, you're the grown-up. You need to be in charge of deciding what's right for you *and* for them.

- *Catch and Release:* If they do cry, hug and comfort them briefly. But then tell them that you're leaving and will see them when you get back. Define this time—in an hour, later that afternoon, in the morning—and be sure to stick to it. Then, come that time, when they see you there they'll realize that you actually mean what you say. Keeping promises like this builds trust and security, and when kids feel secure and know what to expect, they're less likely to feel the need to pitch a fit in the first place.

- *Unplug:* Keep your cell phone handy in case of emergency, but if you want to check in, schedule a time in advance—a mellow, nontransitional moment, like after your kid's in bed—for the sitter to call *you* and deliver an update. Otherwise, you risk interrupting the flow at home and setting off an unseemly emotional scene. You said good-bye before you left, and young kids' phone manners generally suck. There's no need for a "reach out and touch someone" moment.

- *Change the Subject:* When you're out, do everyone a favor and talk about things other than your kid. This will help remind you that you have a life beyond parenthood and force you to engage in the world outside your bubble. But if you do talk about your kid—and you know that you will—try to make an impact. Everyday tales are boring, but everyone *loves* a good disaster story.

SAY "UNCLE!"

2.

Fear of Cheese
Food and Mealtimes

MARTY ARRIVED AT our house bearing coolers. This was something of a surprise to me. I'd driven long distances with Tal's brother before, and the closest he'd come to forethought in terms of sustenance was the purchase of a few bags of spicy Doritos. I attributed the change to his marriage to Cindy, who was also in tow, along with their two-year-old daughter, Brooke. More in character was the fact that the larger of the coolers turned out to be stocked with about sixty iced beers. This would seem a needlessly cumbersome cargo to haul four hundred miles in a car, unless you knew Marty. For Marty, this was "getting started."

The smaller cooler, Marty told us, was set aside for his daughter.

"Let me guess," I said. "Light beer?"

Cindy smirked. She was a driven, right-wing HMO executive—a wild contrast to Marty's "Ralph Nader meets Ralph Kramden" persona—but they seemed to balance each other out as a couple. "Rum punch," she said, holding up a brick of juice boxes. "The forty ounce is more economical, but she prefers the six-pack." She affected a stage whisper. "It makes her feel like she doesn't have a *problem*."

"That's *all* juice boxes?" Tal asked, pointing at the cooler, his tone crossing the border from disappointment to despair. He had a soft spot for snack foods, and I held a hard line against them. Whenever kids came to visit, he hoped for a reprieve.

Cindy peeled back two layers of Juicy Juice, revealing that the cooler indeed contained some foodstuffs, but most of them weren't of the snacking variety. Instead, they were an assortment of processed and prepared meal substitutes: things like frozen mini-pizzas, bowls of microwavable soup, and tubs of reconstitutable pasta. There looked to be enough of them to feed a family of four for two weeks.

"Yum!" Tal said.

I stared at the cooler, which sat on the dining-room table like a blue plastic affront to our decor, and tried to imagine what would possess a parent to drag all this crap with them. I understand that kids need to snack during a trip. When I taught, we brought a portable picnic wherever we went—in fact, having a snack was quite often what the kids understood to be the *goal* of leaving the school. But, aside from an unopened box of orange crackers, the crate's contents weren't heavy on snacks. I also recognize that when parents come to visit us upstate, they want to bring things they believe they'll need but may not be available in our wee rural town: rice milk, organic diapers, insulin shots. But the stuff in the cooler could be found at any gas station mini-mart. I even imagined that they might've wanted to ensure they had some backup meals available—for Brookie, as well as for themselves—in case we'd gone full-force faggot and served nothing but foie gras and caviar. But they knew about my work with young kids; they must have imagined I'd be sensitive to this. It seemed to me that they were Lifeboating.

Lifeboating

Lifeboating is a perilous syndrome, exemplified by a parent's attempt to cart along *everything* their child might need in a given situation: *every* sand toy for the beach, *every* stuffed animal for a sleepover, *every* possible type of clothing for a trip to the park. There's nothing wrong with being prepared. But overpacking is a way of promoting insularity. The goal in leaving the house should be to have your child *experience* the world, not be entirely shielded from it. Moreover, Lifeboating is a way of setting yourself up for failure. Obviously, you can't plan for, or solve, *every* problem that comes along, no matter how focused your efforts. Plus, if you try to, your child will come to expect you to intervene on their behalf—and with a multitude of choices—every time something happens. This behavior prevents them from learning necessary skills—like selection, flexibility, and adaptation—impeding their ability to resolve problems for themselves, and leading to the constant creation of new issues and frustrations: ones they'll expect *you* to take care of. See the cycle? Break it. Bring along only a few choices, and insist that *they* be the ones to adapt. It may take a couple tries for this tactic to work, but your choice here is between a few irritating fits, and a constant stream of them for your child's entire life. You decide.

We found a spot for the coolers out on the porch, and I did my best to put them out of my mind. But my concerns about them came into play almost immediately. Since we assumed that our guests would be hungry after their long drive, we'd set out a child-friendly platter of cheese and crackers, but when Tal presented it to Brookie, she shrieked and pulled away as if we'd offered her a seething dish of botulum toxin. Instead of advising her to calm down, or urging her to try some, Cindy marched to the cooler and dug around for the Cheez-Its. "She's scared of real cheese," she explained.

This process continued throughout the rest of the day. We would present Brooke with a delicious food or drink option—fresh lemonade, veggies and homemade ranch dressing, even brownies—the girl would have a mild conniption, and Cindy would replace the offering with a bland store-bought "equivalent." At some point, I must have made a face, because Cindy clucked her tongue. "Now, come on," she said. "You of all people should know about kids' food."

I'm certainly not one of those people who believe kids should eat everything grown-ups do. Some of the stuff we eat is gross (tongue), pretentious (shallot foam), without value (pork rinds), and/or adventurous for its own sake (toxic blowfish). Still, I made two snacks a day for dozens of kids for many years, and I know that it's possible to get them to eat foods other than those with which they're already familiar. The kids in my school ate curried cabbage, edamame, mango pickle, and blood oranges. And we didn't use tricks, bargains, or bribes to get them to try them. This was simply what we served at snack time, and the kids were hungry, so they had at it. Sometimes they didn't like what we offered, but often-times they were happily surprised. They were particularly fascinated by blood oranges, and for weeks after trying them they

parenting bubble ALERT!

Kids' Food

My work as a consultant for some of the world's largest packaged goods companies has familiarized me with the products that parents call Kids' Food, a category consisting mainly of convenience items that reside in the white or off-white color range (pizza bites, chicken nuggets, string cheese). My research in this world has taught me that young children are often comforted by these foods' mild flavors. But it has also taught me that they're comforted by almost any pasty slurry consisting of fat, starch, and salt/sugar; and it's introduced me to a large number of hugely overweight kids. The goal of mealtime is obviously not to torture your child with grotesque fare like liver or bitter melon. But neither should the core objective be to find dull, nondifferentiable fill just so you can avoid any "blowback." These items can have a place in your kids' diet, but your child's overall food intake can, and should, be balanced. Be aware, however, that you have to be the one to do the balancing. If you authorize your child to lead these decisions, they (rightfully) believe that they're in charge. Do you honestly think your two-year-old is qualified for this job?

requested the *blood* variant of other foods: blood cantaloupe, blood apple juice, blood celery, blood crackers.

Trying new foods also fosters your kid's innate sense of adventure and allows them opportunities to compare and categorize based on prior knowledge (spicy, crunchy, fruit, starch). Perhaps

CHECK, PLEASE

YOUR HANDY CHECKLIST FOR:
Creating Food Balance

Each time you respond to your child's hunger needs, you are creating the nutritional pathways they'll use to serve them in the future. As the grown-up, your job is thus not just to react and respond to what they like but also to craft, shape, and illuminate their understanding of the range of choices. In creating balance, it will help to keep these kid-friendly categories and approaches in mind.

○ *Color:* Food colors are a fun and readily comprehensible way of teaching balanced eating habits. A little white + a little orange + a little green = a healthy meal.

○ *Texture:* You're feeding a child, not an invalid. It doesn't all have to be mush. Mixing textures makes mealtime more interesting. Biting, ripping, tearing, and chewing also help to create diverse expectations from food, a necessity in teaching healthy nutritional balance.

○ *Scale:* Help your child understand portioning and satiation. Start them with small amounts of each of the foods you provide, and teach them to ask for more of what they like or want *if they're still hungry.*

○ *Sauciness:* There is nothing wrong with accessorizing foods to enhance their appeal. Cheese sauce, ketchup, and salad dressing are not your enemies. Just don't let them be your only friends.

○ *Science:* Kids love to dip, cut, dissect, and assemble. This is not *playing with their food,* or if it is, it's fine. Encourage them to sort, make patterns, categorize. But remind them: the end goal is eating.

○ *Skip:* Every meal does not have to come with a dessert. Kids deserve treats, and they're fun for parents to give. But a "treat" is, by definition, something you get once in a while. If it comes every time, it's an expectation—and probably not a healthy one.

○ *Routine:* You know how your child freaks out if you skip a page in their favorite book? That is because it has become a predictable part of a predictable routine. You may have never yet heard your child utter the question "Hey, Mom, where are the vegetables?" But if you make balance a normal and demonstrable part of their mealtime routine, I'm willing to bet that they'll ask for it if it's missing.

more important, exposure to a range of foods informs your child's understanding of appropriate habits of consumption (balance, portioning, satiation, and self-control). A child who is conditioned to consider concepts beyond convenience, comfort, and taste in what they eat will be more likely to develop a healthy relationship with food and less likely to deem it appropriate to pack a lunch consisting solely of rice, popcorn, and cookies (an actual meal I saw a nine-year-old make during a recent research project) or allow two quadruple-cheese Hot Pockets to serve as a normal dinner (ditto for a fourteen-year-old).

Finally, like listening to music or looking at art, exposure to new foods has an intrinsic mind-expanding value for young kids. Food is creative. It is a key signifier of individual cultures, as well as a source of overlap between them. (I once designed an entire preschool curriculum on breads of the world.) It acts as a signpost and a trigger for memories. In our globalized system of delivery, it even tells a story. People can survive for years on liquid nutrition pumped through a feeding tube. It's similarly likely that your child can live solely on PB&J. The question is: is that the only world you want them to know?

While Marty and Cindy relaxed on the porch and drank their beers that day, Tal and I had fun exploring our property with Brooke: taking her out on the lake in the canoe, letting her trample barefoot over the spongy moss, running her through the stream at the edge of the field. She was an adorable toddler, with long skinny limbs and stringy straw-colored hair. In fact, she looked not unlike Tal had in old family photos, and she shared his playful and inquisitive demeanor. Whenever she came upon an unfamiliar object, she would point at it, furrow her brow, and squawk out the invented interrogatory term *"G'noo?"* She was like a puppy, intrigued by everything, sometimes all at once, and we have a number of pictures of her from that visit, squeezing herself into sites she found compelling—the old chicken shed, a milk crate, a dresser drawer, the mailbox.

Given her adventurous spirit, she seemed a natural to be an adventurous eater, but when her dinnertime arrived, and I suggested setting her up with an early-bird version of the meal I was making—tacos, black beans, and avocado salad—I was rebuffed. Instead, out came the frozen mini-pizzas. Brooke had a healthy appetite, and those cheesy little discs were plenty fortified, so I wasn't concerned for her in terms of sustenance. But one of the things that happens to kids who aren't offered opportunities for culinary exploration is that a part of their natural curiosity closes down. Some profound percentage of McDonald's total business consists of people who eat there five plus times each week. I can't help but think that this demographic is disproportionately made up of people who were never asked to grow out of their childish food choices.

Yet for all their apparent weirdness about *what* she ate, Brooke's parents didn't seem to limit her at all in terms of *where* she ate. After just a few squirmy moments in her clamp-on high chair, Cindy lifted her out and set her free, passing her a mini-pizza for each hand. "Don't make a mess," she admonished. I gazed on this scene with abject horror. It was like handing a monkey a blowtorch, and setting him free in a hay barn, with only the instruction "Don't burn anything." Of course, my reaction was blithely ignored. Brookie brushed pizza particles from her shirt, ground them into the kitchen floor, and proceeded to wander about as she ate, getting on and off the furniture, rolling on the rug, and generally placing her greasy mozzarella mitts everywhere.

I was no stranger to people's wide variance in establishing "appropriate" consumption zones for their children. During the home visits I did before each school year (see chapter 11), I had experienced the whole gamut: Dana kept a mound of Cheerios under the blankets at the foot of her bed; Pete ate his afternoon snack off an album cover on which his parents clearly sorted their weed (there was no turntable in the apartment); Irie would have lunch only while sitting on her potty. And I certainly accepted the reality that kids make a mess when they do almost anything. But it is my personal belief that children should sit and eat in a designated area, preferably at a table and in a chair. If they're asked to do so they learn about boundaries and limits. They conform to basic notions of mealtime safety (sitting down while you're eating is much safer than running around). They might even be asked some questions about their day or have other positive forms of social interaction modeled for them. Most important, if they eat in one spot, the mess they make is localized, and you can more easily enlist their assistance in helping to clean it up. This is not only preferable; it is possible. Every day after lunchtime at my school, the kids gathered up their trash and took it to the garbage can. They packed up their leftovers and put their lunch boxes in their cubbies. They helped wipe things down. A select few of them were even graced with a whisk broom so they could crawl under the table and help sweep up. Kids literally *begged* for the chance to be one of the whiskers.

Impossible, you might say, but it's true. Our school cleanup plan worked for three reasons: (1) because it was a part of our routine and thus as regular a part of every meal as eating and spilling; (2) because it was a standing expectation of mine, not a chore or punishment, and kids generally try to meet expectations; and (3) because it was age appropriate and doable and thus satisfying for the kids to participate in. (Plus, I wasn't about to crawl under there—ew!) There's no reason you can't do the same thing at home. Take your kid to the store and have them pick out a little broom set. They don't have to sweep everything—you'd be there all day—but you can expect them to do their share.

Yet even once Brookie's pizzas were mostly gone, and the girl had plopped herself into her father's lap while he read *Popular Mechanics,* Cindy made no move to have her, or anyone else, clean up. I stared suggestively at the trail of crumbs, trying to be WASPily passive-aggressive (instead of my usual Semitic aggressive-aggressive), but it had no impact. When I finally relented and went for the broom, Cindy only shrugged. "Sorry," she said without affect, sipping her beer. "I'm used to having a dog around."

Brookie went to sleep on Marty's lap that night, a position she was clearly used to, because she remained there, prone and undisturbed, through our dinner as well as the start of a noisy game of poker. Marty tried to teach us Texas Hold 'Em, a wildly aggressive variant of the game that had swept the country via the Internet and which, like most trends that originated online, had made celebrities out of a grotesque group of rejects: this one overweight men with wrap-around sunglasses, decal-laden ball caps, and undeservedly smug expressions. (If this is what is meant by a "poker face," deal me out.)

Cindy and I, usually skillful at separating our in-laws from their cash, both lost everything rather early in the game, leaving Tal and Marty to duke it out in a fratricidal frenzy. "All in!" they kept shouting across the table at each other. Fearful that these antics would wake up Brooke, Cindy lifted the girl off her husband's lap and brought her into the guest room. I expected that my sister-in-law would stay in there for a while, getting my niece to sleep, perhaps even falling asleep for a bit herself, and so I took the opportunity to sneak inside and continue cleaning up the food tornado the girl had unleashed. In addition to being compulsive, years of living at our permeable little lake house had schooled me in the industrious abilities of our local vermin. And while Tal, who'd grown up in the country, didn't seem to mind their presence, the peripheral sight of some creature scurrying about, feasting on our scraps, still made me feel under attack.

Cindy came out of the guest room sooner than I expected, catching me scraping a flattened disc of pizza cheese—bearing the imprint of Brookie's toe—off the kitchen floor. She looked at once confused and horrified by my actions, and though my goal had not been to make her feel guilty, I was secretly pleased that this might be a side effect. Yet, instead of acting ashamed or contrite, she simply shrugged, and repeated her earlier comment. "I'm used to the dog doing that." I had to stop myself from barking.

Seemingly reminded of the topic of kids and food, Cindy then launched into a critique of Brookie's eating habits. Not *how* she ate or *what* she ate or—obviously—*where* she ate, mind you, but rather, and rather mysteriously, how *little* she consumed.

"Do you think she's too thin?" Cindy slurred. "She eats like a bird."

You mean she flits around, swallows about a tenth of what she takes in, and shits where she eats? I thought to myself. That actually sounded about right. But what came out of my mouth was, "No. She seems fine." In marked contrast to Marty and Cindy, who had what I'd call beer bods, Brooke was long and thin and had been like that since she was born. "Seems to me, that's probably her natural body type."

"Well, she just had her eighteen-month checkup, and she's in the ninety-second percentile for height but only the twenty-third for weight."

"Long and thin," I repeated, though the whole percentile thing drove me crazy. It was just the kind of quantifiable marker that, while meaningless, worked parents up. "Those numbers aren't a grade. It's not like she got an A for height and an F for weight."

History would bear me out—Brooke remains a beanpole—but Cindy nodded dismissively, and at that moment I could sense where this conversation was heading: into the dreaded PNZ: the *Provision* of *Nourishment Zone*. The staff at my school had come up with this acronym to describe the area surrounding the kids' cubbies during pickup time, and its similarity to the better-known DMZ— the *DeMilitarized Zone*, or no-man's-land, between two warring countries—was not accidental. The designation came about as part of a larger critique, aimed at parents' behavior at pickup time. Despite all of our messaging about this occasion—that it's a difficult transition, an intersection of home and school, that it should be handled gently—the grown-ups often insisted on initiating it with a detective-like examination of their child's lunch box, and a tireless berating of their eating habits. "You only ate half your sandwich?" "You barely touched this cottage cheese!" "You didn't even open your Thermos!" It got so bad, that we started referring to the end of the day, internally, as Pick-*At* Time.

Now, I recognize that there is likely some deep-seated evolutionary link between the provision of nourishment to your child and your sense of worth as a parent. And I know from my own experiences cooking for Tal, that when you go to the trouble of making a meal, a part of you wants the recipient to relish it as if it's the best thing they've ever eaten. But really, people, there's no reason to take it all so personally. And there's certainly no need to make it a standing source of shame for your child. Kids get bombarded with enough confusing food-related messages in our culture. I'm sure you can think of healthier ways of expressing your love.

Like your behavior with most everything else pertaining to your young child, the ultimate goal of your discussions and actions around food is to help your kid develop an honest and reliable internal sense of their needs and to provide them with appropriate tools to figure out how they can meet these needs. So you want to create as straightforward a relationship with food as possible. Laying out clear age-appropriate expectations, having regularly scheduled mealtimes and snack times, and being aware and careful of what you say on the subject are three core ways of attaining this goal. Much of the rest—nagging, begging, cajoling, worrying—is just noise and static. So *stand down!* You are not locked in a battle for survival.

"I wouldn't worry about Brookie," I said to Cindy. "She seems to have a good appetite. I would just be aware of how you use and talk about food with her."

Cindy looked at me as if she was beyond reproach on this account. But as I began describing some of the core food-related no-no's (see Repeat After Me, page 42), she softened—or maybe slackened; she had consumed almost a pony keg of beer—nodding along in recognition, and laughing with particular fervor when I mentioned food bribes and unenforceable threats. "I do that all the time," she said, slamming her hand repeatedly against the table. "Oh god, it sounds so stupid when you point it out."

I smiled with false modesty. "That's what family's for."

thanks for SHARING

One Tiny *GUG* Minute On: Nourishment and Nagging

Kids aren't that good at figuring out very many things on their own, but they're born pretty adept at letting us know when they're hungry (crying), and when they're sated (spitting up). Much of the additional "information" about diet that parents provide after this—dessert as reward, broccoli as torture device, food = love = guilt—only serves to confound this innate sense of balance. Unless your child is suffering from overt signs of malnourishment—weight loss, weakness, palpitations, diarrhea—I suggest you put a moratorium on all food-related nagging. Here are three simple ideas to follow instead.

- Provide sensible portions of a balanced group of foods.

- Distribute these foods at a regular and routinized number of intervals during the day.

- Avoid using food as a bribe, punishment, reward, or weapon (see Repeat After Me, page 42).

How to talk to your kids about: Food

If you're like most parents, you will often find yourself using food as a tool or incentive with your kids. This communicates bundles of bungled information and it is a practice you should take note of and try to correct. Below, you will find a guide to some common (but cruddy) food-messaging strategies, as well as descriptions of why they suck, and examples of why and how to turn them around.

UNCLEAR STRATEGY

YOU SAY . . .

"Eat half your potato, three bites of spinach, and two chicken fingers, and then you can have a third of a Snickers."

"They make sugar from beets, and they make candy from sugar, so you'll like beets."

WHY IT SUCKS:

- This sounds like nonsense to a child.
- All this extra information is indecipherable.
- Food should not be used as a reward.
- Dessert is a treat, not an entitlement.

- - -

WHAT TO DO INSTEAD:

- Provide simple, one-to-one reasoning
- Be confident. You're the grown-up and in charge.

REPEAT AFTER ME . . .

"Eat until you feel full."

"Tonight's Thursday. We only have desserts on Friday and Saturday, and then, only if you finish your dinner."

"These are beets. You haven't had them before, but I think you'll like them. Plus, they turn your poop pink!"

DISCONNECTED STRATEGY

YOU SAY . . .

"Share the swing with your sister or you're not getting any dessert tonight."

"Finish your chicken fingers now or we're not going to tumbling class tomorrow."

WHY IT SUCKS:

- Cause and effect bear no relation to each other.
- Food should not be used as a bribe and/or punishment.

WHAT TO DO INSTEAD:

- Connect invectives and warnings to what's happening, not to food.

- If food is to be part of things, give it a clear reason to be there.

REPEAT AFTER ME . . .

"Take turns on the swing or you're going to have to get off of it."

"Lunchtime is almost over. Finish up so you have time to clean up before tumbling class."

"It's a hot day. Let's get a Popsicle to cool down!"

CONTRADICTORY STRATEGY

YOU SAY . . .

"Have a snack, but don't eat too much, or you won't have room for dinner."

"Come back to the table. You didn't ask to be excused. Now go to your room."

WHY IT SUCKS:

- This is a mixed and conflicting message.
- An inappropriate burden is placed on a child.
- The message creates nonsensical hoops to jump through.

WHAT TO DO INSTEAD:

- You're the grown-up; you do the measuring.
- Keep expectations and repercussions clear.

REPEAT AFTER ME . . .

"Here's a little snack to tide you over until dinner."

"Remember to ask to be excused before leaving the table."

UNENFORCEABLE STRATEGY

YOU SAY . . .

"Stop whining, or you're never having ice cream ever again."

"Eat those peas or we're leaving Florida and going back to New York right now!"

WHY IT SUCKS:

- Cause and effect are unclear.
- The threat is impossible to follow through on.
- Food should not be used as a bribe or threat.

WHAT TO DO INSTEAD:

- The punishment should fit the crime.
- The punishment should be something you can and will do if needed.
- Threats and/or punishments should not include food.

REPEAT AFTER ME . . .

"Whining is annoying. Please use a regular voice."

"You still have some peas on your plate. Do you want to finish them, or are you done eating for tonight?"

REPEAT AFTER ME   REPEAT AFTER ME   REPEAT AFTER ME

Unfortunately, all her banging woke up Brookie, and Cindy rushed into the guest room to comfort her. I could hear her trying to console the girl, and I wanted to give us all some privacy, so I went to brush my teeth. But the girl's crying continued, and as I left the bathroom, I spied Cindy slamming the door of the guest room and heading toward the coolers. I assumed she was grabbing another beer for herself and usefully letting Brooke cry herself to sleep (see chapter 4), but instead she emerged with a roll of chocolate chocolate-chip cookie dough and headed back to her daughter. As she reached for the doorknob, she caught me spying. "She had a bad dream," she explained.

I raised an eyebrow. "Oh yeah?"

Cindy glanced down guiltily at the crumpled tube of dough. "I'll start your no-bribing thing tomorrow, okay? For now, I'm just trying to get us some peace." She opened the door, waving the cylinder. "Okay, Brookie," she said. "I have it. Now, stop whining."

The girl continued sniveling, but the tenor of her cries was almost immediately reduced, likely by having her mouth clogged with chocolatey sludge. "Now you need to stop that whimpering," I heard Cindy whisper, "or we're not going to be able to get this cookie dough ever again." As I turned to head up the stairs, the old floorboards creaked, and I could almost feel my sister-in-law repeating what she'd just said in her mind. "Stop cataloging my mistakes, Uncle Brett," she shouted.

I obliged.

GUG'S *TIPS FOR HANDLING:*

Food and Mealtimes

Mealtimes can be a fun adventure for kids. But, as with everything else, boundaries and limits are needed to help children feel safe and supported.

- *Provide Structure:* When kids know what to expect, anxiety and confusion are minimized, thus reducing opportunities for tension and conflict. Create a mealtime routine with consistent, realistic, and achievable expectations about what is to happen before, during, and after each meal: wash hands, sit down, eat, clean up. Be sure to include a set notion of where each of these steps is to take place.

- *Don't Feed Your Problems:* Most mealtime conflicts are not really about food. They're responses to pressures and situations that surround the event. When kids suddenly "hate" a favorite food it's usually because they're feeling angry, nervous, or displaced. Solve for the problem, not the symptom.

- *Mix It Up:* I'm all about being consistent and letting kids do things again and again. But your child has a better chance of learning to read from hearing *Goodnight Moon* ten thousand times, than they do of learning healthy eating habits from consuming ten thousand portions of pasta. Those green things you've seen in the produce section are called vegetables. If you act like it's normal to eat them, your child will likely believe you.

- *Stay in the Zone:* You don't let your child pee on the houseplants or brush their teeth with the cat's tail. Eating should have its own clear set of rules, tools, and locations as well.

- *Park It:* Unintentional injuries like choking are the top cause of child mortality in the United States. If your child is sitting steadily while they're eating, they're much less likely to have a mishap.

- *Come to Me:* Even dogs know to come to where their food is placed. If you have to follow your child around with their meal in order to get them to eat, you need to ask yourself, Who is their master here?

- *Expect Help:* You can't expect kids to be neat when they eat, but you can expect them to help tidy up afterwards. A one-year-old has no trouble picking up a Mini M&M. This means they can pick up like-size crumbs. Note: wait until meal's end to clean up, or the process may become a distracting game.

SAY "UNCLE!"

Get Stuffed

Buying Things

TAL AND I went down to Key West to visit my sister shortly after our niece was born. With the baby's birth, Roxy and her then-boyfriend Jimmy had decided to tie the knot, and my mom and then-stepfather—a wealthy litigator who'd bought a vacation house in town—were throwing them a party at their beach club. My mother picked us up at the airport, studying our bags suspiciously as we loaded them into her car. "You brought something for the baby, right?"

I shook my head. We'd made a conscious decision not to bring a gift, opting instead to open a bank account for little Amber, hoping to add enough each year to one day allow her to buy something useful: a used car, a semester of college tuition, a nose job. We'd explained all this to my mother numerous times already; she was nagging. I smiled falsely. "I'm sure you've already gotten them everything they need."

"And then some," she said proudly.

We drove to Roxy's cottage, in a charmingly run-down part of town. My sister had never had much in the way of money, but she'd always had a terrific sense of style and prided herself on her ability to put a sweet look together on the cheap. The last time we'd seen her place it had been done in a sort of boho-island chic, with a vintage rattan couch, a Lucite coffee table stacked with 1960s nudie mags, and layers of animal-print pillows, rugs, and throws casually tossed about. It looked a bit like a late-era Rousseau, but it worked for down there, and it was comfortable as hell. So we were more than a bit surprised when Jimmy opened the door.

Gone were the living room's enchantingly eclectic furnishings and accessories. Gone were the contrasting and complementary colors and patterns. Even Jimmy's purple bong, long a fixture by the sofa, had been banished. (I found it later, hidden behind the toilet.) In their place, was a matched group of pale wooden furnishings that looked as if they'd been designed by someone who'd been kicked out of the Shakers for being too bland. This vile collection included a changing table, a bureau, a crib, a playpen, and the clunky gliding rocker on which my sister and newborn niece were seated. The set gave off a chemical smell, like a new shower curtain, and emitted an additional aura of cheapness: like it had been cobbled together out of some flimsy rain forest tree formerly thought to be good only for reducing to charcoal.

Roxy couldn't get up—she was nursing—so we went in and kissed her and the baby. It was at this point that I noted that these furnishings held the additional insult of being upholstered in a watery shade of lilac, a "soothing" color that wouldn't have been out of place in the halls of a nursing home or the powder room of a Connecticut matron.

"Wow," I said. "The place looks really . . . different."

"Mom took me to Baby Warehouse up in Miami. We had to rent a van to get everything back here, and even then we had to strap the roll of carpeting to the top."

I looked down. With everything else that had befallen the room, I hadn't even noticed that they'd covered their Dade County pine floors with a thick layer of beige wall-to-wall. Even Tal, whom I could usually rely on to be gracious, was dumbstruck. "Oh . . . ?" he said, clearly aiming for something resembling interest.

As we chatted and caught up, I moved around, casually testing each of Roxy's new pieces to see if there was some magical benefit that wasn't visible on first glance: if the furniture was actually highly crafted (I saw splinters and cracks), or if it was modular and capable of being infinitely rearranged (it looked more like each piece was planted and would never move), or if it'd been made of some innovative high-tech material that looked hard and cheap but was actually soft and injury-proof (negative). In all honesty, I couldn't find a single motivating reason for such a hideous group of items to occupy a central role in any room, especially a room meant to be the focal point for the absorbent mind of an infant.

I'd been working with kids for a long time and had completed literally hundreds of home visits (see chapter 11), so I'd been exposed to cruddy baby stuff in the past. But the families I'd worked with all lived in tiny apartments, so it was difficult to fit in quite so much of it, diminishing the effect. In addition, I'd never seen these people's places *before* they'd acquired this stuff, so my visits lacked the harrowing impact of the transformation. My sister was one of the first of our family and friends to have a kid, but others were trying, or talking about trying. If this could happen to Roxy, whose motto used to be "fashion before comfort," it seemed it could happen to anyone.

I tried to examine the roots of my horror. I'm not some superficial decor queen—or at least not *just* some superficial decor queen—but I certainly appreciated the fact that the people I knew had panache. It set them apart, made them unique, and I didn't want to see that vanish. More important, it seems that how one

One Tiny GUG Minute On: Parental/Personal Identity

For parents to feel fully engaged in their roles as caregivers, it's of key importance for them to take time for themselves as individuals and to feel entitled to express this individuality. Suppressing key parts of your identity is rarely a good idea (unless the bit you're keeping in check is the asshole part). It breeds resentment, it leads to identity crises, it causes rash behaviors. Look at all those homophobic preachers who are caught sneaking around with male escorts. That behavior is born of a repressed and imbalanced sense of self. Remember, you're not just a parent; you're also a person.

chooses to express oneself outwardly reflects how one feels inside. All of this bland, ugly furniture felt like a way of saying, *I give up—I've had a kid, and now my capacity for connecting to the outside world is over.* This felt like an unfair and unhealthy burden.

As it turned out, my sister was indeed very unhappy at that time, and the phase with the ugly furniture didn't last much longer than her marriage to Jimmy—the rattan emerged from storage soon after he moved out. But as one after another of our friends and family members had kids and ended up purchasing this same ugly crap (and more) I began to feel like something more insidious than identity crises were being perpetrated.

A theory on this had been brewing for some time, but it really hit home following two key incidents. The first came just prior to the birth of our friend Angela's son, Seymour. About two months before the baby was due, Angela received an advice-filled e-mail from a colleague who'd just had a son of her own. Attached, as a bulleted Word document, was a list that had been passed down from another new mother—in a modern take on the oral tradition—and which the friend had apparently used to guide her own prenatal purchases. In fact, she described it as her Baby-Shopping

Bible. The list was titled "The Eighty Things You *Absolutely* Need to Buy *Before* Your Child Is Born.

Receiving the list sent Angela into a panic, not a healthy state for an expectant mother. Not only did she not have most of the items it contained, there were a good number of them—things being touted as *required for the practice of modern parenthood*—that she'd never even heard of before. It is not a stretch to imagine what something like this would do to the self-esteem of a person who was already sleep deprived, desperate, and hormonally imbalanced. Picture a card house collapsing.

Angela was prone to hyperbole, and since she never mentioned the list again, we allowed it to remain in the realm of urban baby legend. That is, until our friends Kate and Dylan were eight months' pregnant with their firstborn and received a copy of the exact same list. It apparently had one of those Internet curses attached—you couldn't show it to anyone but a new parent, or some horror would befall your child—which explained why I hadn't actually seen it. But when we stopped by to meet little Max for the first time, I had the ulterior motive of observing how its advice had played out.

Dylan answered the door and led us into the apartment. He had been raised in New York and had been fortunate enough to inherit the lease on his grandma's rent-controlled two-bedroom, uptown. The second bedroom, which had previously housed their home office, had been converted for Max's use, and though the little bugger was nowhere to be seen, we immediately noted the transformation here: their stylish "Louis XIV meets Louis Kahn" workplace aesthetic had been supplanted by a duplicate of the ugly set I'd seen at my sister's. "At least the door closes," I muttered to Tal, as we made our way into the living room. But as soon as I said this, I spotted the glider rocker planted by the couch. It seemed to wash up at the house of every family with a newborn, like condoms on the beach in Cancún. Worse than this was the marked absence of the piece of furniture it had supplanted, Dylan's favorite recliner: a stylish, commodious, and inexplicably comfortable La-Z-Boy that he'd always referred to as a "family heirloom."

"Can I ask you something?" Tal held a finger to his chin. "Where's the baby?"

"He and Kate are getting ready," Dylan said.

I had no idea what this meant. What does a baby get ready for? It wasn't like this was his debutante ball or something, but Dylan didn't seem open to questions. Instead, he led us to the far corner of the living room, which had also been given over to infant-product creep, and began demonstrating another host of new purchases. "These must be from the list," I stage-whispered to Tal, hoping to incite our new daddy to confess. But Dylan kept mum, displaying each item with the kind of reverence straight guys usually save for power tools or home-theater equipment: "Check out the easy open-and-close hardware on this changing table." "Peep at the ingenious integration of this recessed baby wipe holster." His tangible sense of excitement almost made us feel guilty.

This being America, where you are what you buy, it seemed clear that much of the affection Dylan displayed for these new purchases was connected to his affection for his newborn son, so there was something tender buried within this frenzy (even if it involved redundant items like the baby-food blender next to their Cuisinart, or the baby-bottle warmer plugged in under their microwave). We even smiled generously through his show-and-tell. That is, until he introduced us to the Diaper Genie.

The world is now familiar with this marvel, but at that point we hadn't seen one, and Dylan demonstrated its action. "You put the used diaper in here," he said. "Then you just twist with one hand, and, voilà, it's gone."

Tal took on a bewildered expression. "Where does it go?"

"The diaper? Inside. They get . . . wrapped up."

"In what?"

Dylan paused. " . . . Plastic," he said, just like in *The Graduate*.

"Why not just use a shopping bag?" I said. "That's what we used when we changed kids at my school. The parents were thrilled to bring them in and put them to good use, as everyone seemed to have a drawer or closet stuffed full of them. I personally can't leave the apartment without acquiring at least two."

Dylan shook his head as if we were philistines. He pointed at the Diaper Genie. "These are odor protected. They use a technology that seals the smell away."

Neither of us had the heart to tell him that this was decidedly not the case. We had both noticed, on entering the apartment, that though the living-room windows were open, what Tal's mom refers to as a "septic scent" pervaded the air.

Tal and I stood there in horror, a sensation made all the more acute when Dylan opened the top of the Genie to prove just how functional it actually was. Curling around the inside of its cylindrical body, like the guts erupting from some cheap sci-fi movie monster, was a string of what looked like shit sausages. I nearly threw up in my mouth. The whole concept seemed idiotic. We have an effective and extant technology for handling this situation: it's called a garbage can. One can be purchased with a tight-fitting lid, and the contents of it can be emptied as often as necessary. We don't have dedicated receptacles for every other kind of stank trash—Salmon Skin Genie; Empty Cat-Food Can Genie—I don't see cause to invent one for this.

Around this point, Kate finally emerged from the back bedroom with Max. She always looked good—she had modeled as a teen— but she looked radiant and voluptuous in that way new mothers often do. Still, she did not seem to be in a good mood, and though we made a big commotion over the baby, everything we did seemed to try her patience. "I'm sick of this," she said, throwing herself into the rocker and glaring at her husband with something resembling rage, as if the entire situation was part of some plot he'd been hatching against her, and which had, just then, reached its fullest fruition. "I've been trying to nurse in there, and it's just not working." She then said the six strangest words I'd ever heard her speak. "Dylan. Get me the Boppy cushion."

Having worked with kids as long as I had, I didn't expect to be surprised by *two* infant accessories in the same day, but indeed, it happened. Dylan knelt down at the far end of the couch and retrieved a peculiar C-shaped pillow, and while Kate held Max aloft, he wrapped it around her waist. It looked like a soft-sculpture version of the trays worn by cigarette girls in old movies, albeit without the shoulder straps, or the cigarettes.

Kate caught me staring as she laid Max on this shelf and attempted to guide his head toward her nipple. She shot me a glare. "Don't. Say. Anything."

Given the strain on her face, and her direct admonishment, I managed to keep my big monkey mouth shut. But as I watched her struggle to accomplish whatever she was trying to do—feeding, I believe—my gut theory came into focus. Kate and Dylan, and the other new parents I knew, were indeed battling a vicious campaign: being stripped of their confidence in their ability to conduct the most basic business of rearing a child and made to feel inadequate and incompetent. And this war was being waged not by their mothers or mothers-in-law, as it had in the past, but by the very products they were purchasing to "help" them. Now, I'm not some sort of cantankerous Luddite, opposed on principle to new technologies. And I understand firsthand the subtle pressures of marketing (I'm a marketer after all!) and how they can work on new parents, who only want the best for their babies. But I believe that women all over the earth—and even right here in the United States—have been successfully nursing for years without the use of a Boppy cushion. And I think these kinds of "tools" have only one message for parents: *you are an idiot, and you have no idea what you're doing.*

It took K&D about three weeks to stuff the Boppy cushion into the Diaper Genie and toss them all in the Dumpster. I'm unsure how much longer the other seventy-eight "necessary" items lasted.

parenting bubble ALERT!

Parental Infantilization

Following in the footsteps of the wedding industry, the baby industry is becoming ever more adept at marketing and selling you items you don't need. But unlike the wedding racket, which seems to play on your fear that you're going to spoil your one shot at perfect memories (*Don't you think your vision of matrimonial posterity should include hand-lettered place cards laser embossed with your image?*), the baby business seems to play on your fears that you're ill equipped for the job and are going to do it all wrong. It's a kind of consumer infantilization that I find totally disempowering and counterproductive for parents. I'm sure there are people out there who feel rescued by the Boppy cushion. But before you buy one, or anything like this, I want you to think, What is this product trying to tell me about my capabilities? No wonder we have a generation of parents who have so much trouble being the grown-up. Everything they buy is telling them that they're a bunch of silly little babies.

But you don't have to make the same mistakes they did. You can empower your inner parent and not buy this crap in the first place. Use your brain, or the handy checklist below, to make sensible substitutions that draw on your own innate skills, and save the money you would've laid out for something useful, like a babysitter.

In addition to this movement toward infantilizing parents by rendering them reliant on hordes of silly products, there seems to be a correlative trend toward overendowing kids with too many toys, clothes, and things of their own. Again, I'm not at all opposed to buying stuff, and I know that there's nothing like the rush one gets on delivering a gift to a child, but there is something to be said for moderation and perspective.

Nowhere was this practice of overstuffing more evident than in our good friend Danika's apartment in Chicago. It was a big, rambling prewar space with a long hallway leading off to generously sized rooms, but despite the grand scale, it could barely contain its sprawl of kids' stuff, which emanated—like an unsealable leak— from our "niece" Erica's enormous bedroom. (Like any good contemporary parent, Danika and her husband, Josh, had given their daughter the master suite.)

Tal and I had a special bond with Erica, and as soon as we arrived at their place, she would grab our hands and usher us toward her room. No matter what time of year we arrived, she always seemed to have just received a windfall of gifts, and approaching this end of the apartment would always put me in mind of how my ancestors must have felt coming upon the Red Sea; I feared we'd be engulfed.

"Come with me," she said during one particularly memorable visit, taking our arms and marching us toward her lair. We passed piles of tiny dolls and discarded Day-Glo clothes, which littered the floor like casualties of some failed campaign: the Polly Pocket! Crusade. And when we finally made it to her room, she had to

CHECK, PLEASE

Baby Product Substitutes

Here are some of the products from the list of eighty "necessary" items and some readily available household goods you can use in their stead if you'd like to pretend that you're the grown-up.

"NECESSARY" ITEM	GUG SUBSTITUTE
○ Diaper Genie	○ Garbage can
○ Boppy cushion	○ Lap/Arm/Pillow
○ Baby-food grinder	○ Blender
○ Nursing glider and ottoman	○ Chair/Rocking chair
○ Infant in-crib sleep positioner	○ Mattress/Rolled-up towel
○ Digital bath thermometer	○ Finger/Wrist
○ Temperature-sensitive feeding spoon	○ Finger/Wrist
○ In-sink baby-bath holster	○ Kitchen sink
○ Six-drawer multilevel changing table	○ Flat surface (counter, table, floor); towel
○ Portable infant dinnerware set	○ Plastic take-out container and spoon
○ Baby-bottle sterilizer	○ Soap and hot water
○ Tub-side kneeler	○ Folded towel
○ Cuddly fleece baby receiving blankie	○ Cotton blanket
○ Baby wipes warmer	○ Lobotomy
○ Handbook for expectant moms and dads	○ *The Gay Uncle's Guide to Parenting*

shoulder the door to get it to open, revealing a seething, foot-deep mass. It looked as if Santa's sleigh had done an end-over just out of the gate at the North Pole and rained down its transglobal contents just there. But rising amid this chaos, barely visible across the room, was a rounded pink hump, a pair of green pajama bottoms flying from its summit like a flag. "My new tent!" Erica howled. "Let's go inside."

The girl scrambled over the morass with ease, like an Andean mountain goat traversing her native terrain, but Tal and I found the crossing significantly more difficult. We had a hard time distinguishing between stable ground and potential hazards, and our stockinged feet kept plummeting through the crusty epidermis and striking objects in the magma below: a Barbie leg, a tambourine, the moldy remains of a sandwich.

Since the tent was brand-new, I somehow imagined that it would offer refuge—a Zen temple amid this unwavering chaos. But as Erica unzipped its flaps, we found that this was not the case: it was literally full to bursting as well. "It's my toy box," the girl said, a concept that made about as much sense in that room as a sandbox in the middle of the desert. But since we'd reached our ostensible goal, I thought that we could now settle down to play. Yet when I asked Erica to pick out something that she wanted us to work with, her eyes darted around glassily, as if she was unable to see a single option.

Our friend Danika had grown up the only child of two ascetic architects, so though she'd spent her childhood in the mercantile hub of Chicago, her parents had shunned consumer culture. She was raised in an industrial neighborhood that not only lacked a Kids "R" Us, it was almost entirely lacking in *kids,* and when she would ask her parents for a toy, they would either look at her like she'd lost her mind or build her an ersatz simulacrum in their studio. During the heyday of handheld Mattel electronic games, she was given a piece of painted wood rigged with a battery and two LEDs.

I felt for the way she'd been deprived as a kid and the manner in which—like many parents I knew—she was attempting to make up for what had gone wrong or missing in her own childhood by doing the exact opposite with her daughter. Still, given Erica's inability to see the forest for the trees, it seemed a better balance could be struck.

One solution to this problem is to focus your purchases on simple materials that can be used in a wide variety of ways. This limits the number of choices your child has to confront, while simultaneously expanding the options for their utilization. For example, when buying materials for my school, we purchased only items whose use was open-ended: wooden blocks, pieces of fabric, arts and crafts supplies (paint, paper, markers, scissors, glue), clay, water and sand toys, and manipulatives (LEGOs, Bristle Blocks, K'NEX). A toy plane can only be a plane. But because open-ended materials have no inherent function other than as creative tools, kids can engage with them without the limitations of fixed or solitary uses. In other words, they can be used

thanks for SHARING

One Tiny GUG Minute On: Kids, Things, and Choice

No one wants to be that parent that's known as a killjoy—the kind where the only "toys" in their playroom are a deck of cards and a chessboard. At the same time, there's such a thing as having too much stuff. Young kids are only capable of comparing a finite number of choices: two is optimal; three is pushing it. So when they're confronted with a room full of options—be they toys, food, or clothes—their processing system short-circuits, and they have a very difficult time focusing and making effective choices. This issue is compounded by the consistent addition of new items. Not only does this add more "noise" to the decision-making process, but if a child grows accustomed to this constant flow of goods, they may begin to assume that the only worthwhile choice is that which has been added most recently.

to make just about anything. These materials thus encourage kids to analyze ideas and parse them into their basic elements *while they play.* A table is made by creating a flat surface (a spread-out cloth); a house by building an enclosed space (an open square of blocks); a city by lining up a colonnade of buildings (a row of blocks). These materials encourage kids to return to them again and again, bringing not only new experiences but also new skills and abilities into their play. (Note: the same is true of clothes, where basic separates can be combined in myriad ways, instead of relying on dedicated "outfits.")

It may seem counterintuitive, but by simplifying and limiting what you offer your child, you're actually opening up the possibilities for their use and expanding the options of what they can explore. By using simple open-ended materials, you place the onus on your child to be creative, imaginative, and thoughtful in how they approach things, empowering them to be the ones to design and execute meaning in their play (and life). The children in my class literally made everything in their world—and some things that were out of this world—from these kinds of materials: beds, skyscrapers, jackhammers, aliens, dollhouses, trees, post offices, spiderwebs, rocket ships, dinner parties, skis, harmonicas, computers, maps, fire trucks, dentists' chairs.

Of course, I recognize that this is something of an ideal: your kid is going to want other things, and on a certain level they deserve them. But again, remember, you're the grown-up. It is not only within your power to decide how many or what kinds of toys or clothes or foods your child is going to have around, *it is your job.* Setting consistent and meaningful limits creates security for young children. It also makes exceptions to the rules all the more special. And, as I've said with regard to other parenting issues, it's never too late to make a change. Just because your child's closet is already stuffed with clothes they don't wear or toys they don't play with doesn't mean that you have to go on buying more. You can decide to stop, simplify, or pare back at any time. Just be sure to involve your kid in enforcing the decision. Don't quit cold turkey without saying anything. And don't remove all your kid's stuff one day while they're at school. Explain things, describe your goals, and get them to help you carry them out.

For example, after becoming annoyed with the amount of junk in her house, my sister Roxy placed a moratorium on all new purchases and combined this with a culling of her daughter's things. Once a week, for about a month, she'd enlist Amber's help sorting her toys and clothes into three piles: things I never use, things I sometimes use, things I use all the time. The first pile—often containing items still in the bag in which they left the store—was unequivocally given to charity. The second was granted a reprieve and stored in the shed until the next round. The final pile was returned to the girl's room, so long as a proper and practical storage spot for it could found. While it's been a struggle for our niece to let things go, and for my sister to stick to her guns and not buy more, they're both happier with the result. Roxy said that the girl is now much less likely to say "I'm bored. What should I do?" or "I don't know what to wear," and much more likely to be a self-starter and stick with her choices.

Of course, while you may be the primary source of stuff in your kid's life, you're not the only vehicle by which it comes into your home. There are relatives and friends, birthdays and holidays, the dreaded goodie bag. But don't fear, you have options for dealing with these as well. You can enlist the support of the people in your life by laying down some ground rules and asking them to conform—blocks only; no costumes; stocks and bonds always welcome. Don't be afraid of doing this. It's your right. (If your child had a nut allergy, you'd find a way to let everyone know not to offer them cashews!) Another choice is to stick to your rules at home, but allow other locations—like Grandma's house, for example—to have freer rein, kind of like those orthodox Jewish families I know who keep kosher in their own kitchen but scarf down bacon whenever they eat out. Or you can use some combination of these two ideas, where *you* buy only what *you* want for your child but allow friends and relatives to give the little darling whatever catches their eye.

Remember that no matter what you decide, this is an ongoing process; you'll need to keep working at it, refining and adapting as things change. Also remember, this isn't just about decluttering. It's about thinking of how best to benefit your child's (and your own) ability to focus, make informed choices, engage with the world, and use things practically. We all see more clearly when there's less haze and smog interrupting our view.

GUG'S TIPS FOR HANDLING:
Buying Stuff

Many of the products out there for parents and young kids are junk, and the supply of them is endless and overwhelming. It's important to think about the following issues before you buy.

For You

- **Is It Me?:** In this culture, you are what you buy. So before you make a purchase, I want you to ask yourself, Do I really want to *be* a tacky, three-foot-tall, white plastic diaper bin? It may be hard to find parent stuff that reflects who you feel you are, but don't stop trying or you risk losing yourself.

- **Limit Choice:** Neither you nor your child will be happier or more fulfilled if you have fifty different kinds of sippy cups, or underwear, or cereal in the house instead of just two or three. Endless choice is overwhelming for kids—and for adults. Keep it simple.

- **Look for Multiple Uses:** A Diaper Genie cannot act as a trash can once your child is out of diapers. But a trash can can. Seek out items whose life can be extended and can be used in more than one way.

- **Protect Yourself:** Marketers are expert at playing on your fears and insecurities. (Trust me, I am one.) Think long and hard about buying or keeping any product that makes you feel inadequate, desperate, or panicked every time you use it. Raising kids is hard enough. Spare yourself this additional drama.

For Your Kid

- **Think Open-Ended:** Play is how your young child explores and makes sense of the world, so it's worthwhile to consider the tools you provide to serve this function. Open-ended materials like blocks, manipulatives, and art supplies push kids to be more active participants in constructing knowledge.

- *Skip the Weapons:* Is a gun really the kind of tool you want your child to use to explore and construct their knowledge and sense of the world? I hope your answer is no.

- *Make Rules:* You're the grown-up. You make the rules about what comes into the house. Limits create a comfort zone for kids, so the more clear you are about these rules, the more secure your child (and you) will feel, and the less likely you'll all be to desire or buy stuff you don't actually want around.

- *Stand Firm:* Remember, if you give in to guilt or whining, kids (rightfully) believe that these are successful strategies. If they guilt-trip and whine and you don't respond, the lesson learned is that these tactics do not work (see Appendix, page 231). Which do you prefer as a long-term goal?

- *Don't Be Draconian:* We all deserve *some* crap in our lives. Simply practice balance and moderation: allow your child to explore the toy aisle for five minutes every time you go to the store, but let them know that they can only pick something to purchase once a month/season/year; let them select one junk-food item every time you visit the grocery store; allow them to choose their dress-up outfit for a special occasion (birthday, Halloween, Uncle's Gay Wedding).

SAY "UNCLE!"

4.

Don't Go in There

Crying and Bedtime

DYLAN LOOKED EXHAUSTED. He and Tal and I were at The 212, a dark hotel lobby bar in an obscure corner of Manhattan that had little to recommend it besides the fact that we'd been going there forever. Dylan and his wife, Kate, had first taken us there at least a decade prior—long before they'd been married or had kids— and for about five years it had been the site of a weekly rendezvous that usually ended with at least one of us prone and babbling. It had been many months since we'd had a proper binge with either of them, and while drinking to excess is clearly a strange thing to feel nostalgic for, we'd recently developed this sense of longing whenever we saw Kate or Dylan: a wistful yearning for the days when they were a bit more unencumbered.

Almost as a reminder of how things had changed, after an initial bit of catch-up, the conversation shifted to the cause of Dylan's fatigue: lack of sleep. Sleeplessness, in my and Tal's life (and in Dylan's past), was usually connected with debauchery, and I hoped against hope for a juicy story—a drunken flirtation with a

colleague at his social service agency, a sex-filled anniversary cele-
bration, a rekindling of his teenage love affair with LSD—but it
quickly became apparent that this wasn't the case. "It's Athena,"
Dylan said flatly, naming their seven-month-old daughter. "She
won't stop crying when we put her down. I honestly think that she
might have some kind of disorder."

I nodded, aiming for sincerity. I'd recently dealt with another
friend whose son was having trouble sleeping, and after I'd flip-
pantly advised her that there was likely nothing wrong, a specialist
found the boy to have a mild case of sleep apnea. "So," I said,
"what are her symptoms?"

Dylan looked into his drink. "Um . . . crying, mostly."

Thinking I might be able to satisfy him with a diagnosis of
colic—which is merely a folksy way of saying your baby was born
cranky—I asked him to elaborate. "Well, how long does she cry for
before she falls asleep?"

Dylan squinted. "What do you mean?"

"I mean, for example, a colicky baby will often cry for hours on
end. So when you put Athena in her crib, and she cries, how long
does she cry without stopping?"

"I don't know," he said sheepishly. "We haven't gotten that far
yet."

Tal skewered an olive with his drink-stir. "That far in what?"

"The program. The *sleep program* we're using." Dylan rolled his
eyes. "Jeez. You guys are so out of it. We're doing the Ferber process.
We're Ferberizing her."

I widened my eyes, marginally insulted at how entombed my
parent friends could become in their PARENTING BUBBLE—acting
as though their "discovery" of some theory for dealing with kids
marked its literal entry into the world. I'd earned a master's degree
in education. I'd run a successful preschool. I knew who Richard Fer-

ber was. He'd been around since the 1980s, preaching the sensible gospel of training parents to let their kids cry themselves to sleep. "I'm familiar with Ferberizing," I said. "So, where are you at with it? When did you start? How long are you leaving her alone for?"

"Right now, we're trying to pass the quarter-minute mark."

Ferber usually worked in larger increments than this—something more likely to be measured on a wall clock than on a Olympic stopwatch—but Dylan mentioned this duration the way a drag racer speaks of the ten-second quarter mile, as if it was some mythic goal that required technical mastery, relentless training, and a bit of divine intervention. I was stunned. "And exactly how long have you been working toward this objective?"

"Probably three weeks, give or take. To be honest, Kate usually starts to guilt-trip me after about ten seconds, staring me down, blocking my view of the TV, saying things like 'Are you going to go and rescue your daughter or not?' Her efforts tend to escalate from there until I either give in and go and get her, or Kate storms off to get her herself."

"And then what do you do with her?"

"I don't know. Take her out of the crib, walk her around, put on some music—she loves Earth, Wind and Fire, or anything with a big horn section. Sometimes Kate feeds her. Sometimes we bring her into bed with us."

I stared blankly at my friend but eventually managed to compose myself. "I hate to break this to you," I said, placing my hand over Dylan's, "but that's not Ferberizing. In fact, that's not even in the same galaxy as Ferberizing. It sounds more like the sleep deprivation tactics the army's been using in Guantánamo. I want to ask you a serious question: did either of you actually read one of Ferber's books?"

"Kate said she read it cover to cover. But she said the same thing about *The Corrections,* and she never got even halfway through that. I only read the checklist thing at the back."

"Well, that explains your focus on this so-called fifteen-second mark." I held my drink-stir to my mouth as if it was a pipe. "I belieff," I said, affecting a Viennese accent, "dat *you* are de vones who haff de sleep disorder." I pointed at Dylan. Both he and Tal winced.

The goal of the Ferber method isn't to teach you how to use a timer. It isn't even really about training your child to go to sleep. It is, like much of what I advocate here, about teaching you as parents to take a step back and think about your child from a rational perspective—not as an extension of your ego or sense of self-worth but as a human organism struggling to develop. In this, its core objective is to help you learn that when your kid cries, it doesn't mean that (1) they're dying or (2) you're a bad person.

Young kids have only a few lines in their job description: eat, observe, sleep, pee/poop, and cry. This is not that many choices in terms of how to spend the day, and so in order to keep things interesting, they'll often mingle two or more of these actions (observe and cry, sleep and pee, eat and observe). But regardless of how many potential combinations exist, there is only one choice here that represents a means of communication: *cry.* So when faced with most any unfamiliar situation, and almost every situation for them is unfamiliar—they *were* just born after all—they use this method to "talk" to the people around them.

Now, we as grown-ups generally cry only when we're unhappy and, even then, usually just when we're very unhappy. That is in part because we have, over the course of our long and tragic lives, developed all sorts of other sophisticated means of dealing with our essential needs. If we're hungry, we can order Chinese. If we're thirsty, we can mix ourselves a cocktail. If we're tired, we can drink an energy beverage. If we miss our mommies, we can call them (and realize, shortly after they answer, that we don't actually miss them all that much). Though it's decidedly un-American and a sign of weakness that gives strength to our enemies, we can even talk things through, admit mistakes, or ask for help. But— and please write this down— *young kids aren't just little grown-ups.* Their brains fire differently. They haven't developed language. They have no teeth! Therefore—in much the same way that teenagers seem to have thousands of uses for the bland term *word,* each with its own distinct inflection and definition— crying can mean many different things for babies, and very different things than it does for us.

Given all this, like nearly everything else with your young child, the objectives when dealing with crying at bedtime are threefold:

- To assure your child that you love them and that you're there for them.

- To let your child know that you are in charge and know what you're doing (or at least to act as though you know more than they do).

Crying

Young kids have few options for expressing themselves. You know what they do have? Crying. So when they cry, it's not just because they're hurt or upset. They cry because they can no longer see whatever unfamiliar object they were just observing (the coffee table, a pizza box, your fat lazy cat) and they're puzzled by its disappearance. They cry because you've been carrying them around all day, and you've put them down briefly to answer the door and flirt with the UPS guy. They cry because you've ceased cooing and making idiotic faces at them for one second so you can go into the bathroom and pee. Please note: *these are not traumas.* They reflect a response based on a limited palate of options. It is your job, as the grown-up, to teach your kid about the existence of other options (gesturing, talking, denial). It is your job to teach them how to find their center and learn to solve their problems on their own. It is also your job to let them know that every time they start crying, you will not drop everything and come tearing across the house as if they're on fire. At some point in their life—and the sooner the better—your child needs to reach the end of their rope and see that life continues once they get there. Otherwise, they'll never learn where their rope ends, and you'll be left holding on to it for them . . . forever.

- To help your child learn to find their own personal center so that they can develop practical and functional responses and move on.

All of this takes time to learn. But, as with spanking your child in order to teach them to exert self-control over their behavior (see chapter 7) or forcing your child to finish a giant portion of pasta in order to get them to understand their appetite (see chapter 2), picking your child up—or panicking, becoming anxious, or otherwise losing your mind—every time they cry at bedtime is not an effective method for teaching them how to relax and fall asleep on their own. It is, in fact, antithetical to this goal. It breaks the cycle of independence and creates a cycle of dependency wherein your child never gets a chance to realize that they're going to be okay, or to figure out how to soothe themselves, because they're always expecting you to step in. Think of it this way: do you think it would be an effective means of enhancing your professional growth if every time you had difficulty with a project at work, your boss came into your office, grabbed the job from your hands, and completed it themselves?

I gave Dylan a condensed version of this spiel. "You need to let her cry," I said pointedly. "For longer than fifteen seconds. For longer than a few minutes, actually. Though it can be hard on parents, I often recommend just closing the door on the first night, and letting the kid cry until she falls asleep: it works like magic. But feel free to take it in increments—significant increments, like, in the two- to five-minute family. And when you do go in to check on her, leave her in her crib. Step in, reassure her, and then close the door." I nodded. "Come on. I mean, you've been through this before, right? When Max was a baby? He sleeps through the night now. How'd you make that work?"

Dylan shrugged. "I actually have no idea how we solved things back then. The whole time from his birth until age two is a sort of a blur. It was like we were part of a stand-up team, forced to improvise our act based on phrases hurled at us from the audience." He stared at his empty drink glass, his face sinking further. "Plus, whatever success we had back then has been lost now. With all the noise Athena's been making and all the attention she's been getting, Max has started this new routine of refusing to stay in his room at night. He'll wander out when one of us is trying to calm her down, and rile her up, attempt to draw away our attention by doing something naughty, or insist on being coddled. We'll tuck him back in and tell him to stay, but he doesn't listen. The other night, Kate had to stand outside his door for forty-five minutes, holding it shut from the outside while he screamed and struggled to yank it open. He finally passed out, right on the floor. I couldn't even open the door to put him in bed."

Tal and I were speechless. Tal's mouth was actually hanging open, like a character in a Bugs Bunny cartoon. I was tempted to reach over and close it, but that seemed egregious. I went for the rational approach instead. "Sounds like letting Athena cry herself to sleep will kill two birds with one stone then. It will help her learn to get through the night. And it'll eliminate the incentive for Max to seek negative attention."

Dylan waved me off. "Whatever. It'll be fine. It's probably just a phase." He shook his head. "I mean, I know you dealt with lots of crap at your school. But, not to be disrespectful or anything, you never really had to handle bedtime."

Dylan was right. My school didn't have a real bedtime. But we did have an enforced rest time for thirty-plus kids every day, and the same tactics we used can be applied at home. Getting a kid to go to sleep (and/or stay in bed), like most everything else with young children, is about the establishment of expectations and routines. *Expectations and routines are like a staircase that descends into the desired behavior or activity, one predictable step at a time.* They create an insulating sense of comfort and familiarity for your child, especially during transitions. Since the transition from waking to sleeping can be a particularly scary one for young kids, especially once they begin to understand what it means—blacking out, losing control, having the familiar world vanish—easing into this with a proper lead-up is acutely important. You should establish a consistent but gentle protocol, one that allows for downtime (a bath), a strategic sense of choice ("Which of these two books do you want me to read first?"), and firm statements of intent ("Once we finish reading, I'm going to turn off the light, and kiss you good night"). Ownership over an event breeds confidence and comfort so you should also let your kid share in age-appropriate responsibilities (turning pages, putting on their pajamas).

For example, at my school, we would lay the cots out in rows, and after each child finished eating lunch and cleaning up (see chapter 2) they would get their blankets from their cubbies and make their beds. Some kids were meticulous about how their covers were laid out, some heaped them in a pile and burrowed under, but everyone knew that it was their job to set things up. The kids were allowed to wind down in a sort of half light before rest time officially started—looking at books, chatting quietly, or just talking to themselves—but once the five-, three-, and one-minute warnings had been delivered, they all knew they were expected to lie down and be quiet.

We would read a couple picture books, just to get everyone in the mood, but when the remaining overheads were clicked off, every child would either go to sleep or rest quietly for at least an hour. To help them make this transition, the teachers would gently rub each kid's back for a couple minutes. A few might occasionally cry or act out, especially during the first weeks of school, and we would comfort and reassure them. But this didn't excuse anyone from rest time. We would tell them, as we would if they cried over our daily venture to the park or what we were having for a snack, "I can see that you're upset, and I'm sorry that you're feeling that way. You can cry about this for as long as you need to, but this is what we're doing right now, and I'm not going to change my mind." Ninety-nine percent of the time, they'd cry it out, and move on.

Of course, this leaves the other 1 percent of the time. Samirah's behavior fell into this tiny minority. She was a legacy at the school, the younger sister of a wonderful girl named Nikela whose parents— a West Indian painter and an Irish housing rights advocate—had become friends of mine. This meant that Samirah had been a part of the school community for her whole life when she started in the inaugural class of our new two-year-olds program, a fact that some-how fed her spirited and mischievous temperament.

I had hired a fantastic teacher named Roberta to oversee the new group, and while she and I would touch base regularly I delegated all day-to-day authority to her. This meant that I was spared the gory details of who tussled with whom and what everyone built in the block area. But since Roberta had the odd habit of talking at a superfast clip, and often when she was walking backward and away from me at day's end, I sometimes missed some of the relevant bits of her progress reports as well.

One of these bits apparently concerned Samirah's behavior dur-ing rest time, an issue that didn't become clear to me until I entered the two-year-olds' room one afternoon, looking for fruit for our postnap snack. All the cots were lined up and occupied by placid toddlers—like a bunker full of new soldiers just before the hazing rituals begin—except one, which was off in the corner behind the easels. I could tell right away that it was Samirah's, not simply because of the presence of her Kente-cloth blanket or Nikela's hand-me-down stuffed leopard. The main giveaway was the fact that Samirah was clinging to one leg of the cot, howling, while Roberta clutched at the girl's feet, shaking her—seemingly attempting to separate child from bed in a manner usually reserved for flinging the kink out of a garden hose or liberating a staticky sock from a freshly dried towel.

"Roberta . . . ?" I said, using my best teacher voice, a tone meant to communicate my dissatisfaction with a behavior, while leaving the responsibility for changing it up to the person in question. But caught in a TEACHER'S BUBBLE of her own, Roberta didn't reply. Eventually, my presence forced her to take stock of the situation, and she set Samirah's feet down. Not wanting to shame her, I asked for the fruit and then suggested we talk later that afternoon. "But I think it's best if, in the meantime, you discontinue whatever you were doing over there."

Roberta came up to my office once the day had ended and, after a general apology, explained the situation. As it turned out, Samirah refused to rest at rest time and had been waging a war of attrition over it since the first week of school. Roberta had tried all sorts of appropriate responses—setting limits, stating expectations, giving chances, following through—but each was effective for only a few days, before the girl would start some new disruptive behavior. Roberta sighed. "I keep having to come up with increasingly vehement strategies."

"So that's what I was witnessing down there? A 'strategy'?"

"She'd been lying under her cot, kicking at it, all through rest time, and it kept waking Angelique—who's a bear and whose mom gives me hell if she doesn't nap. I gave her three warnings and told her that if she didn't stop, I was going to have to put her back up top myself. *That's* what was happening when you came in." Roberta smirked. "I would have had her too if you hadn't interrupted. She was growing weak, I could tell."

I laughed. I adored Roberta's dark sense of humor, but like most people who worked in early childhood, she was a bit of a control freak and sometimes needed to be reminded when to let go. I remembered something my mentor had told me during my first year in the classroom, when I'd been engaged in a protracted lunchtime battle with an evil three-year-old. "Have you ever heard the sound of one person fighting?" I asked.

Roberta sighed. "Is this some sort of passive-aggressive Zen bit, Brett? Because I'm tired, and I'm nearly late to meet my boyfriend for a drink."

"It's not Zen." I grinned. "It's a . . . *strategy*. For guerrilla warfare with kids."

Roberta curled her lip. She was a punk chick from the heyday of the East Village scene. She used to date Joey Ramone. She didn't take a lot of shit. "Sounds Zen to me."

I explained the tactic: a type of targeted disengagement. "Just give her enough room to fuss and then ignore her," I said. "I promise she'll soon grow bored and stop."

"I'd rather build her a cot with a lid," Roberta replied. But I trusted her enough to be certain that she was listening.

I knew that there was nothing worse for an experienced teacher than being too closely supervised. I also knew that implementing a change like this takes time. A classroom is like a construction site in this way; it seems all chaos and wallowing in a big muddy pit, and then suddenly something solid begins to rise from the foundation. So I waited a week or so before popping by at rest time. Samirah was nothing if not tenacious—fighting for primacy against her perfect older sister, she'd probably been like that since the day she was born—and I doubted that she'd be sleeping peacefully. In this,

I was correct; she was sitting bolt upright on her cot. But instead of behaving disruptively, she had gathered a large pile of picture books and was taking up each one, flipping through it thoroughly, and then depositing it in a discard pile. Though I could tell it was a struggle for them both, she and Roberta were doing an excellent job of ignoring each other.

"That was her interpretation of my suggestion that she read some books to occupy herself during rest time," Roberta whispered. "She's been on every corner of that cot this week, trying to get my attention—under, over, standing, turning flips—but I've been playing it cool. It's taken more willpower than quitting smoking, and I doubt she'll ever go to sleep, but this is what she's settled on for rest time."

I glanced cautiously at the girl. "It looks restful," I said.

"Yeah, sure. For *her*."

I nodded. *That's what we're going for,* I thought to myself.

We moved on to other topics that night at The 212, letting the subject of bedtime drop. And the next few times we saw Kate and Dylan, they didn't talk much about their kids. Tal and I enjoyed the adult-centric nature of these outings, and even broached the possibility among ourselves that we were getting our best friends back: that they were emerging from their PARENTING BUBBLE to become normal humans again. But as with folks we knew who were involved in rocky relationships, we weren't sure whether their failure to mention the kids meant that things at home were on an upswing, or that they'd devolved to a point beyond polite mention. Being selfish about our time with them, we didn't ask.

I assumed that the situation had changed for the better—it sounded like it would have been difficult for it to have gotten worse. I was therefore shocked by the bedtime debacle we witnessed when Kate and Dylan came to visit us upstate that summer.

On the phone before departing, they sounded like they had a functioning system in place. They intentionally left the city late, just before the kids' bedtime. They brought along books on tape and a portable DVD player to help the little darlings drift to sleep in the car. They even claimed to have given them a half dose of cough syrup—the good kind with alcohol and drowsifying decongestants. But when they got to our place at 10 p.m., both kids were not only wide awake, there didn't seem to be any plan for putting them down. First Dylan made a big show of setting up Athena's crib in the guest room, while Kate sat in the car with the two screaming kids. Then they put the girl in there on her own and let the boy tear around the house wreaking havoc. Then they sent Max in there with his sister, but he pinched her and she started crying, so they let him escape and run around some more. Then he got overtired and whiny, so they gave him some cookies and warm soy milk. Then, finally, they shut them both in and closed the door.

One Tiny GUG Minute On: Bedtime Battles

For most kids, a loving Ferber-type method is enough to help them learn to sleep through the night. But some kids—the stubborn, the mischievous, the truly evil—require more attention. These are the kids who, instead of simply crying, seem to constantly find new ways to instigate or call you to them. If you've been sucked into one of these bedtime battles you may want to reevaluate your rules of engagement. A key tactical change includes *ignoring your child's antics*. You'll still need to state your expectations, but then you'll need to give your kid some room to rail against these strictures, allowing them space to work out how to accomplish this goal. Remember that your child is seeking your attention, so if you make each of their moves into a struggle—checking up on them constantly, nitpicking their every effort—they'll quickly realize that this is a prime way to get what they're after. Instead, be firm and clear—and then walk away. If your child reacts, respond by calmly restating your expectations but do not reengage. They'll soon learn that it's impossible to have a satisfying war with only one combatant.

I breathed a sigh of relief and starting pouring the martinis. But though the business of the evening seemed done, and we were all together on the porch, our friends remained distracted. Kate didn't even sit down. Instead, she stood near the door with an ear cocked to the wind. She poked Dylan angrily. "She's crying," she said.

Dylan took a sip of his drink.

"I said, she's crying."

Her husband shook his head. "Don't go in there."

"She sounds miserable."

"Don't go in there."

"She'll keep him up."

"Kate. Sit."

No longer able to restrain myself, I set my drink down. "Don't they share a room at home? Haven't they worked all of this out?"

"*They* who?" Dylan said. "I don't hear anything but the crickets."

Kate remained standing, glaring at her husband.

Athena's cries waned and finally seemed to disperse. But though Tal and I made increasingly desperate attempts to initiate conversation, our friends remained too engaged in being angry with each other to participate. This made me realize something essential about parenting: that bad parenting decisions—especially monumentally bad ones, ones that if looked at objectively for even a second would appear as ridiculous as trying to stop a runaway elephant by jutting your leg out to trip it—are often made not out of lack of knowledge or an inability to focus but because inertia and oppositionality trump people's ability to behave rationally. Kate and Dylan had each started down a path, and neither one of them was willing to step off.

True to form, Kate soon stormed into the house. I heard her pause at the guest room door—a Ferber tactic. "It's been a year of Ferberizing," I said to Dylan. "How many seconds are you up to?"

He gave me the finger.

A moment later, Kate reappeared holding Athena. The girl was wide-eyed, taking the situation in, trying to reconcile the strange surroundings. "She just wanted to see what was going on, didn't you, girl? She hates to miss anything."

Dylan rolled his eyes. "Who doesn't?"

Kate gave him the finger. And then, as if to prove some point, she kept Athena up for almost an hour, switching her from knee to knee and shoulder to shoulder. We hadn't seen the baby in months, so it was fun to note how she'd developed, becoming more and more herself. But this practice had me worried about the next two nights. I wanted to ask our friends if they really believed that taking their child out of her crib, showing her an entirely alien location, and parading her past a crowd of near strangers was really an effective means of helping her get to sleep. When I have insomnia, the last thing I believe will help coax me into slumber is leaving my bed, flying somewhere I've never been, and interacting with an unfamiliar group of locals.

"Isn't it time to put her back?" Dylan said, crunching his last ice cube.

Kate sneered. "She's almost ready, aren't you, sweetie?" She bibbled the girl's lip with her index finger. "But if she cries when I put her down, you have to promise not to gloat."

Dylan crossed his heart exaggeratedly. But, true to his word, when Kate emerged from the guest room and Athena immediately started bawling, he remained silent, calmly cracking open pistachios. Eventually, the girl was joined by additional caterwauling from Max, who, while likely capable of falling asleep to his sister's constant drone, had clearly been awakened by her sudden intrusion. "Daddy!" the boy cried. "Dad-dy. Da-ad!"

Kate gestured toward the guest room. "Your son is calling you."

Dylan exhaled angrily and set his hand on the arm of the chair, preparing to pull himself up, while making it clear that if he did, what happened in the guest room would not be pleasant. "Don't make me come in there!" he shouted sharply.

The kids silenced themselves, as if considering this threat. And then, realizing this engagement was exactly what they desired, they began screaming in unison, even louder than before. Dylan shot up, and Kate stood and ran after him, like some 1940s film heroine, ready to throw herself between her children and her husband's murderous rage.

"*They* should write a parenting book," I said. "It'd be a Greek tragedy."

Tal nodded. "Among some tribes in Africa," he said sagely, "children are never separated from their parents, not even for a second. They're carried around everywhere. I saw it in a documentary." He paused. "I wonder . . . Do you think the kids cry like this there?"

I shook my head. "If you had to be with your parents twenty-four hours a day, don't you think you'd become adept at ignoring their insanity?"

"Good point." Tal grabbed the shaker and cocked his ear toward the door, where we could now hear our friends shouting at the kids *and* at each another. "I'll go make us more drinks," he said. "If they ever come out of there, we're all going to need them."

GUG'S TIPS FOR HANDLING:

Bedtime

Getting your child to sleep on their own can be difficult for parents and kids alike. But once it's properly taken care of, I guarantee you that you'll feel liberated. Try implementing these simple steps.

- *Make a Routine:* Start with the time right after dinner, and come up with a list of what needs to be accomplished in your evening. Then create a realistic schedule for completing each task. This isn't the military, so you don't need to time each act down to the minute, but remember: consistency makes things easier. You can even ask your kid to help with this list, but be sure to veto any submissions that smack of delay or distraction (calling Grandma, reading fifteen stories, waiting for the eleven o'clock news).

- *Spell It Out:* Provide reinforcement by telling your child how you expect the night to run. "We're going to do X, then we're going to do Y, then I'm going to say good night." Once they're capable, have your child tell *you* what comes next. This way, the routine will become theirs as well.

- *Be Positive:* Phrase your expectations in the affirmative, providing your child with a road map of what you *want* them to do, rather than pointing out only what you *don't.* Say "You need to stay in your room" instead of "Don't even think about getting off this bed." This gives your kid a model of how to please you instead of detailed pointers on how to get your goat. (See chapter 6.)

- *Give Assurance:* Your child will ask *why* they need to go to bed. Make sure you provide a real explanation. Tell them that they need to sleep to be healthy and ready for the next day and that you need private time to work, think, and sleep as well. "Being an exotic dancer is physically demanding. Mommy needs her beauty rest."

- *Where Is the Love?:* When you say your final good night, make sure you let your child know that you love them and that you're going to be around to ensure nothing happens. Kids often have irrational fears about bedtime: that you're going to leave for a party or a trip to Mars as soon as they fall asleep. Burst these bubbles without blowing any new ones.

- *No Last Chances:* When you close the door for the final time (literally or figuratively), make sure you mean it. If there's the opportunity for one more kiss/hug/glass of milk, your child will take advantage of it. They don't do this (solely) to be annoying; they do it because you've told them that they're allowed to. Decide what you'll tolerate and then stick to it.

- *Tracks of Their Tears:* Your child might cry. They might cry *a lot*. But you need to stand firm. It's their job to learn how to find their center, and it's your job to provide a platform for them to practice this. This is one of the most important skills your child will acquire, so know that you're not an instrument of torture; you're simply doing your job as the grown-up. If the sniveling goes on for an extended period of time, you can go in, commiserate, and reassure. But no new chances or stories or bringing them out to kiss the dog. You open the door, you say your piece, and you close it again.

- *Give It Time:* Like cement, new routines take time to set, so don't expect a miracle on the first night. This is especially true if other things are in flux (and they often are). And be prepared to be annoyed. Your kid will probably come up with a stream of irritating responses, so get ready to ignore them.

SAY "UNCLE!"

5.

I Want to Eat It

Toilet Training

TAL AND I had learned from experience that, like when approaching an unfamiliar dog, the best practice with parent visitors is to remain motionless and let them come to you. So when our friends Bridget and Esther arrived at our house upstate, we stayed on the screen porch, tidying up and arranging the hummus platter Tal had set out. Though these two ladies had been together for years, they hadn't ever been to our place in the country. Much of this was my fault. Tal and Bridget had been friends since college, but she and I had always had something of a contentious relationship: I was too sharp-tongued, and she took me too seriously. But she'd apparently relaxed since she'd borne their son, Teddy, so when their weekend invitation was announced, I promised to behave.

Though we were all in our thirties—our *very* late thirties—Bridget's youthful persona remained delightfully unchanged. She still sported a coal black Elvis-inspired haircut and a hawkish expression that somehow conveyed both certainty and vulnerability. I'd only met her girlfriend, Esther, once before—at Teddy's first birthday party the previous March—and knew little about her save that she was Korean, taught high-school biology, and had a taste for gin, and that Tal had, more than once, described her as acerbic. It always intrigued me that the people who complained most about my cutting wit tended to select partners for themselves who shared this trait, but sensing an opportunity to divide and conquer, I'd stocked up on Tanqueray.

I had a clear sight line to the driveway, and I could see that even by modern standards—what I like to call No Child's Toy Left Behind—our guests had an astonishing amount of baggage. Most intriguing among their possessions, and the one that was first to be unpacked, was what looked like a tiny pink plastic chair. Esther handed this to Teddy—rather sternly, I thought—and had him carry it on to the porch.

I knelt down and reintroduced myself. "Hi Teddy. I'm Brett."

"Hello, Mr. Brett," he croaked loosely. He had a voice like a cartoon turtle, wore a Molly Hatchet T-shirt and a pair of yellow board shorts, and in addition to his chair, held tightly to a ragged stuffed owl. I loved his whole look.

I pointed to a child-sized folding chair Tal and I dragged out whenever we had kids up, to prove to our young guests and their parents that *we care.* "I'm glad you brought your own seat," I said, "but we already have one for you. See?"

"His is a potty," Esther said flatly. She had small oval glasses, a blunt ponytail, and was wearing a wife-beater and cargo pants. She looked like a drawing of a lesbian. She pointed at a spot less than a foot from where I'd set out the food. "You can put it down right over there, Ted-o."

I was a bit stunned by the suggested proximity of crapper to hummus, but it gave me a chance to study the contraption. It was a nearly radioactive shade of pink, with a contrasting tangerine-colored bowl, and it was covered with decals of a furry red character, clearly meant to evoke Elmo from *Sesame Street*. It was the kind of potty one might buy from a street vendor: the fake Louis Vuitton bag of the toddler set.

"Nice toilet," I said to Esther, attempting to lure her onto my team.

"This? Ugh." She rolled her eyes in Bridget's direction. "*She* picked it out."

"I told you, *Teddy* picked it out. Now let it go, will you? The store was next to my studio, the price was right, and we needed something quick for this goddamn trip."

I felt mildly insulted. "This 'goddamn trip' up here?"

Bridget sighed and explained. Apparently, they were using their weekend with us as the jumping-off point for a six-week visit with her parents in Vermont. Esther was going to teach summer school there, and Bridget planned to start some new paintings. They would use the grandparents as live-in babysitters while they worked. It sounded like a recipe for disaster to me. Bridget's folks were sharp-tongued and she took them too seriously, resulting in their having a contentious relationship. (Are you detecting a pattern here?) But in their drive for unencumbered time, I'd seen parents make more desperate bargains than this. Tal's sister sent her six-year-old to sleepaway camp. My own sister allows *our mother* to take my niece on monthlong road trips.

As they removed Teddy's diaper and sat him on the potty, they informed us that they'd meant to begin the toileting thing months before but had lost focus until recently.

"So . . . when did you end up starting?" I asked, delicately.

Esther shot Bridget another look. "Yesterday. Well . . . today, really."

One Tiny GUG Minute On: Starting New "Projects"

We've all been amazed (and seduced) by how receptive and adaptive kids can be when new things are presented to them on the fly—foods, activities, Mommy's "special friend." But a project like toilet training constitutes a major life change for them, and such things benefit strongly from being introduced in a familiar, low-pressure environment. Imagine trying to learn to drive a stick shift while vacationing in Rome or giving up drinking while visiting your parents. Sure, it could be done (for example, if you happen to travel with a Valium drip), but the odds are stacked against you. Your child will be more likely to succeed if such efforts are initiated within a comforting and "normal" context. This provides the supportive scaffolding, security, and confidence that kids require to attempt adaptation. Starting a new project in a strange environment has the potential to produce anxiety and shame—for your child *and* for you—and is a recipe for conflict and battles of the will. It should be avoided whenever possible.

Teddy looked none too happy about being stripped of his Dora Pull-Ups and asked to sit on the potty in front of two near strangers, a situation made all the worse by a few additional factors: (1) his mothers were standing over him, expectation plain on their faces; (2) he'd been cooped up in a car eating popcorn and dried fruit snacks all day and was probably in mild gastric distress; and (3) he could now see, from where he was sitting, the brightly colored kiddie pool we'd set out for him in the side yard.

I wanted to offer some advice. But given our guests' clear investment in this project, the negative history I was trying to erase, and my desire to provide Teddy with some semblance of privacy, I went for distraction instead. "Hummus, anyone?"

The dip worked like catnip on our Sapphic sisters, calming their nerves, and harnessing their attention away from their son. We sat around the table and began discussing Bridget's new pieces—a series about the indignations of being a pregnant butch lesbian. "One would think," she said dryly, "that a waitress wouldn't address a woman in her ninth month as '*sir.*'" But we were able to remain focused for only a moment before we spotted Teddy running to the far side of the porch and clambering up on to the rickety camp bed there. He began bouncing, while seated, clearly attempting to corral his moms' attention, but they weren't biting and I was impressed by their ability to ignore his antics: to allow him to be harmlessly silly without intervening, letting him know that he was not the only center of their attention. I did spot Esther sneaking a peek at the potty, which, from my vantage point, appeared predictably empty. But just as she was about to answer Tal's question about the school she'd be teaching at, her expression seized up and she stood and walked toward the seat, staring down at it in silent horror as if it had grown lungs and begun to breathe. It wasn't until she slowly moved it aside, that we were able to see the source of her piercing terror. Somehow, in the few seconds of "privacy" we'd provided him, Teddy had managed to get up off his potty and squat alongside it, and he had laid a giant turd right there on the floor. It was brownish green and marbled, like a bad cut of meat, and was roughly the size and shape of my forearm.

"For the love of God," Tal said. "How the hell did that come out of him?"

"More important," I said, "how are we going to get it off our porch?" I pointed at the phone. "Call Tim, and ask him if he can bring over his tractor."

"Guys," Esther said quietly, gesturing over at Teddy, who, having rid himself of what appeared to be his ingrown twin, was now beaming brightly and rolling around bare-assed on our quilt. "I think you're making him feel bad. We should be celebrating."

"We should be fumigating," I corrected. Teddy seemed fine. And regardless of what he'd extruded, it hardly merited rejoicing. "In case you didn't notice, he missed."

Esther shrugged. "But not by much."

Forever the voice of reason, Bridget asked for some cleaning supplies. "And I'll need a plastic bag or something—forceps—to pick that up."

Looking diminished, Esther walked over to Teddy, and began stroking his head like he had a fever. "What are you going to do with it?" she asked her girlfriend.

"Why? Do you want it for the baby book? I thought I'd toss it into the woods."

"I see. So *that's* how you want to teach him to deal with his poop?"

"No. *That's* how I want to get it *far away from us.*"

"Well, I think we should put it in the potty and have Teddy bring it into the bathroom. Then he can dump it in and flush it down, just like they do in *Dora Poops.*"

I wanted to veto this idea—frankly, I feared for our plumbing—but I had to admit that Esther had a point. Modeling normative behaviors like this is important in establishing new routines for kids. It calmly shows them how to deal with what can be frighteningly novel situations. But I definitely did not want to be involved. I'd once had to walk a good friend's dog and to lift his steaming shit off the sidewalk with only a latex glove for protection. The whole situation was giving me retching flashbacks.

I retreated to the kitchen and watched from there, and I was impressed by the ladies' efficient division of labor: Esther transferred the log from floor to potty, and Bridget doused the whole region with a fine misting of Pine-Sol. Teddy smiled gleefully at the ruckus he'd made, which seemed a warning sign to me. And though he showed absolutely no interest in flushing his poop, they all gathered in the bathroom and made a big production out of doing so, as if holding a wake for a beloved pet fish. My gag reflex had finally diminished—until I heard them washing the bowl out in our bathtub.

Though we spent the rest of the day out in the yard, the potty remained firmly planted on the porch and was referenced somewhat threateningly throughout the afternoon, as a combination historical marker and warning beacon. "I can see your pot-ty," Esther singsonged from the pool. "Teddy has a pot-ty," Bridget echoed later, over iced coffee. It stayed there through cocktails and dinner, and even after Teddy had gone to sleep, as if by moving it we might alter some now-perfected routine.

By the time Tal and I got downstairs the following morning, Esther was already out in the pool with Teddy, and Bridget had brought the coffeepot onto the porch and was reading an old *US Weekly*. We grabbed some mugs and joined her. Since the weather had continued to hold and the sky was crisply blue, we were both a bit surprised to find the floor glistening and damp. "What happened?" Tal asked. "Did it rain?"

"So to speak." Bridget sighed. Teddy had apparently taken another crack at the potty that morning, attempting to pee this time. Thankfully they'd insisted he go sitting down, and he'd managed to land most of it in the bowl. But, no doubt delighted with the response he'd commanded the previous day, once he finished, he'd stood up, pulled out the reservoir, and proceeded to empty it onto our porch.

I looked around in mock panic. "Where's the potty now?"

"I put it in the car," Bridget said. "I think we'll try this again at my parents'."

"Do they have a porch?"

"They have a sunroom," she said. "Carpeted."

I curled my nose. "You know, this may not be the best time to start this process."

Bridget nodded. "Yeah. I know. But we have all this time together, and we really need to get it taken care of before the fall."

I had encountered this idea of parents getting something "taken care of" by a certain point many times before. These deadlines were usually set based on some checklist they'd seen in a book or Web site or some urban baby legend they'd heard inside the PARENT-ING BUBBLE. "We'd really like her to be walking by nine months." "We hope he'll be talking in sentences by one." "We'd like her to get into Yale by eleven." These kinds of time-coded goals always seemed counterproductive to me. I believe that if they're considered at all, they should be viewed as rough generalizations or averages. And it should be recognized that as *a human individual,* your child doesn't adhere to rough generalizations or averages. Few developmental milestones occur on their own, so it's your job to provide the necessary guidance. But remember, there are no extra-credit points awarded—in their IQ score, in heaven, or on their college applications—if your child is toilet trained at age 2.7 versus age 3.

I wanted to ask Bridget, "What's the rush?" But Teddy slipped and fell getting out of the pool, and she ran over to him and Esther. I went inside to make some drinks, and the next time I looked out, they were huddled around their son, encouraging him to pee, standing up, in our bushes. "I'm not sure if he's doing this right," Esther said, pointing at his penis. "Maybe we can get one of the guys to come out and show him."

I didn't volunteer. I personally believe that boys should be taught to pee sitting down. It limits the worries about aim, some studies say it's better for the bladder, and if universally adopted, it would finally rid us of that tedious seat-up/seat-down battle that every sitcom writer seems to think is the pinnacle of comedic genius. I pee sitting down most of the time myself. It's relaxing. More than this, toilet training, like everything else with young kids, benefits from being taught in a consistent manner, and this whole in the potty/in the woods, sit-down/stand-up business seemed anything but regular. I said a little prayer for the carpet in Bridget's parents' sunroom.

SINCE OUR FRIENDS all had children at roughly the same time, they're all experiencing their kids' developmental milestones simultaneously as well, so it wasn't too surprising, later that month, when we got an emergency toilet-training call from Kate. We were in the car at the time, on our way to visit her and Dylan, and Max (age 2.10) and Athena (age 1.3), at a lake house they were renting about an hour northwest of us.

"I need you to get some underwear," Kate said sharply. "Something in three-year-old size. Preferably with Batman or Spiderman on it."

"We're in Liberty," I said. "There's nothing here but pawn shops and titty bars."

"I'm sure there's a Target or Kmart nearby. Stop at a gas station and ask."

I paused for effect. "You want the two of *us* to go into a gas station in rural upstate New York and ask where we can find some little boys' underwear? I hope you have bail money; we'll end up in jail." I rolled my eyes at Tal, who was driving at the time. "What's the emergency anyway? Can't you just wash the ones you have?"

"He doesn't *like* the ones we have. He refuses to wear them. This is a crisis."

I heard Max shrieking for Pull-Ups in the background. "Should I call UNICEF?"

Kate sighed. "Just get the underwear. And some wine. Lots of it."

Attempting to kill two birds with one stone, we stopped at a fancy liquor store in Deposit, intending to inquire where we could find some little-boy panties. But even here, with an obvious city transplant behind the counter, the question seemed loaded. "Can you tell us where we can buy some children's . . . socks?" Tal asked.

"Socks?" The clerk widened her empty eyes. "Are you making puppets?"

Tal touched the neck of the wine bottle. "How much for the rosé?"

From what I knew of Max, I didn't think he was ready for undies anyway. He was a bit of a slow starter temperamentally—slow to walk, to talk, to sleep on his own—and he struck me as the kind of kid who didn't like to be rushed. But Kate was clearly dead set on getting him trained—she called two more times before we arrived, and she grabbed my arm as soon as I walked in the door. "I can get him to sit on the potty," she said. "But I need you to tell me how I can make him push."

"Make him push? You have control issues."

She squeezed my wrist tighter. "Tell me!"

She was clearly too far gone to listen to my patented strategy, which, like most of my strategies for working with kids, involved equal parts *patience, routinization,* and *the provision of limited options.* For example, in dealing with toilet training at my school, we simply had mass bathroom breaks four or five times a day, where everyone in the class sat on the pot, regardless of whether or not they thought they had to "make." This familiarized the kids with the idea of a regular lavatory schedule, gave them loads of real-life practice with the equipment (theirs and the plumbing's), and showed them that the bathroom program worked if they worked it—all removed from any sense of pressure or emotion. It was just another part of the daily routine. Though a number of kids always started school in diapers, by the end of October nearly everyone was out.

"You need to relax," I told Kate. "Let's go for a swim."

The house they were renting was right across the lake from a summer camp, so every half hour or so, a recorded version of "Reveille" would play over the loudspeakers, followed by garbled directions regarding the next scheduled activity. Kate told me that when they'd first arrived, Max had been frightened by the noise, but he now perked up and did a little dance each time the tune played. He'd become even more *dramatic* since the last time we'd seen him: his moves looked like something from a bad drag routine.

Tal and Dylan took the boy out for a ride in the rowboat, and as we watched them paddle around, Kate continued to quiz me about toileting. I told her about my patience/routinization/low-option strategy. "So that works for *everyone*?" she asked.

"Almost," I said. "Some kids need a little extra push."

As an example, I told her the story of Yitzak. Yitzak was a bit of a worrier—he was one of the few three-year-olds I've met who actually wrung his hands—and though he'd shown an interest in using the toilet during the fall, with success he'd become scared and had retrenched. Come spring, he was still wearing diapers all the time. Kids, especially nervous kids, often have a hard time giving up vestiges of their babyhood; they worry that the adults in their lives are no longer going to take care of them (see chapter 10). So, despite my best efforts to reassure him, Yitzak held out. The situation eventually began getting in the way, especially in terms of his social development. Wearing diapers at his age carried a stigma, and even his closest friends—a gregarious boy named Ian and a nearly feral girl named Aja—had started to pull back. As a defense mechanism, Yitzak had taken on the personality of a cat, crawling around the classroom, hiding behind shelves, and responding to all questions solely in *meows*.

I knew that Yitzak was a smart and observant child. He had great ideas and excellent problem-solving skills. I also knew that he was physically able to use the toilet. He had simply fallen into a shame spiral. He was embarrassed that he was still in diapers and was becoming increasingly afraid to reach out to his peers because of this, and all this concern and confusion fed on itself to fuel this distance. I called his parents in for a conference. They were academics and refugees from the former Soviet Union and were highly resistant to any "mandated interventions" in their son's development. But I told them that he needed their help. I said that letting go of this last public remnant of infancy is incredibly important for a young child's creation of an independent sense of self and for the promotion of their social persona. They worried that he wasn't ready.

"He told us that he wasn't," the father Avram insisted.

"When he tells you that he's a cat," I said, "do you believe him?"

I gave them a simple, straightforward solution. "Tell him that in three weeks you're going to get rid of all the remaining diapers and that you're not going to buy any more from then on. Involve him directly in the countdown however you can: have him cross the days off the calendar, have him pick out underwear he likes, have him come up with a list of times he can practice using the bathroom. He's ready. He just needs you to be the grown-ups and give him a nudge, to provide him with some direction and guidance."

Kate listened attentively to the story. "Did it work?" she asked.

"Pretty much. He had a number of very public accidents during the first week or so, but that's normal, and his peers were totally forgiving. But once he got it down, he was like a different kid. His block buildings gained complexity, he cracked jokes during story time, his playdate calendar maxed out. He even started walking upright."

"So, I can do that with Max? The countdown thing?"

"I don't think we're anywhere near that point yet."

"So then, *what,* Mr. Potty Man?"

I stayed on message, once again stressing routine and detachment, two things I knew Kate wasn't particularly good at. She was the kind of person who would never order the same entrée twice and would always get the waitstaff involved in her decision.

"That whole protocol thing just seems so . . . boring," she said, slamming her head back for emphasis. "It's like he's punching the clock or something."

This was an issue I'd heard parents express before but never with such openness and conviction. It was a poignant insight into a foreign mind.

I tried to explain a child-centered vision of routines to Kate but was interrupted by the camp's loudspeaker. Kate pointed as Max performed his little dance in the boat, and as I watched I noticed that his movements were smoother and more refined than before. My friend seemed surprised and pleased at this growth, and it struck me to use this performance to make my point. I described how, now that Max was totally familiar with the bullhorn song, he felt free to try out new and more sophisticated movements in response. "Routine is like that for kids. It's a stable structure into which they can root their imagination."

"So I should make him try to shit every time that song plays?"

parenting bubble ALERT!

Routines

Parents want to keep life *interesting* for their child, and since grown-ups equate routine with drudgery, they often resist consistency for its own sake. What's missing here is the understanding that for young kids nearly every lived moment involves something novel and *interesting* and that this constant barrage of new information requires a stable template through which it can be organized and explored. A routine isn't boring to a young child: it's terra firma. This is particularly true when they're trying to learn a new skill. If the tools they're using are familiar and predictable each time, they can focus on the task at hand without being distracted by other noise. For a young child, an unfamiliar bathroom is like a foreign landscape. You see a green toilet; they see a monster. Routines are grounding and necessary for kids. Don't fear them.

Kate sneered, but I knew she was listening. She resisted new input; we were similar that way.

"What's the big rush anyway?" I asked. "Aren't you guys on vacation?"

She nodded. "Yeah. But we need to get this taken care of before the fall."

"That's what Esther and Bridget said. Are you all reading the same guidebook?"

"No, stupid. Both our kids are starting school in September."

I sat upright. "You mean they have to be toilet trained *before* they start?"

Kate nodded. "That's right. At the school Teddy's going to, if a kid has an accident, their parent has to leave work and come to the classroom to change them."

I shook my head in wonder. As I've said before, kids develop at different rates, and so I don't agree with having firm and inflexible rules about when they should achieve things like being fully toilet trained—especially at just over age two and a half. I had no rule like this at my school. It was like having a rule about when children were supposed to start speaking in sentences or when they should begin understanding metaphor. But if that was my friends' reality, I figured they could do worse than to follow my strategies. I looked at Kate. "Lucky I got here when I did."

Kate tried to demonstrate that she'd internalized my advice by insisting that Max sit on his potty a few times that afternoon. Of course, she alternated between yelling at him to hop on and not following through, skipping both the emotional divestment and routinization pieces. But later, after we'd had a few bottles of wine and were immersed in adult conversation, Max dragged his potty over next to the picnic table where we were sitting and without much drama squatted down and pushed one out all by himself.

Kate and Dylan sprang up and knelt beside him, smothering him with hugs and praise. They even insisted that we join in a round of applause. Tal set down his glass and leaned toward me. "We're clapping for shit," he said. "How'd this happen to us?"

Once the ovation died down, Max squatted down to consider his achievement, studying it closely for quite some time. Freud says that kids think of their shit as a gift to their parents, an indication of their accomplishments—much the same way that cats think of those headless creatures they're forever leaving in their owners' shoes. But apparently Max had other ideas in mind. He looked up at his father. "I want to eat it," he said.

"Now, Maxy," Dylan said, as if they'd gone over this a million times. "What will happen to you if you eat your poop?"

Max pondered this question. "I'll get sick?"

"That's right."

The boy nodded, and reconsidered. "I want to touch it."

Dylan sighed and looked at me. "May I have some more wine, please?"

"I have a less disgusting idea," I said, thinking of Bridget and Esther. "Why don't you take it into the bathroom and have Maxy dump it in the bowl. Then you can practice the whole post-toileting process. He can wipe himself, flush, and wash his hands."

I was pleased with myself for incorporating our friends' struggles into my own programmatic ideas, but I still must have managed to come off like an expert because Kate rolled her eyes. "Know-it-all," she said.

GUG'S TIPS FOR HANDLING:

Toilet Training

There is no "magic bullet" for getting your kid to use the bathroom. Like everything else in a child's development, it's a process. And like any process, to achieve stable, long-term results (as opposed to short-lived, short-term stopgaps) it requires planning, persistence, conviction, and forgiveness.

- *Don't Wait / Don't Push:* You can familiarize your child with the toilet—what it's for, how it's used—long before they're ready to use it themselves. Let them sit on it, let them flush it, let them see an older child use it. Casually develop their interest, *without pressure*.

- *Prime the Pump:* Toilet training is not going to happen on its own. You'll need to be proactive and take the lead. You know your child. Follow your common sense. Remember how you knew when was the right time to encourage them to try going down the slide on their own? This is like that.

- *Routinize:* Once you're ready to start training in earnest, pick a number of relevant times during the day—first thing in the morning, after dinner, right before bed—and make getting on the toilet at those times part of your routine. Remember, a routine is something that is done *regularly* and *consistently*. If you offer it up as a choice or pose it as a question, it's no longer a routine; it's an option.

- *Present Limited Choices:* You're a parent not a dictator; you have to be capable of flexibility. So if you need to present options, make sure that all the choices you give are ones you find acceptable. "After you finish eating breakfast, it's time to try using the bathroom. You can either go in there as soon as you're done, or once you put on your shoes. Which one?"

- *Divest:* Routinization helps remove emotionality from a situation. That's why the assembly line was invented. Think of yourself as the factory foreman: you're there to lay out a rational and efficient process. If you freak out every time someone tightens a bolt, the car will never get built. Also, a good foreman knows that workers deserve praise for their successes, while guilt, shame, and coercion only produce confusion and anxiety. It's piss and poop, not life and death.

- *Provide Incentives:* Make a chart where your kid gets to put up a sticker each time they use the toilet. Make four-page potty books where they can draw pictures and dictate the story of each successful visit. Let them pick out their own panties, ones they like. Make it fun.

- *Be Patient:* Other toilet-training methods might be faster—prohibiting your child from wearing clothes, never changing their diaper—but expedience is not always most effective (or healthy) in the long term. *This process is not linear, and there will be accidents,* but your child will ultimately learn to find their center, develop pride in their abilities, and understand and respect your expectations.

SAY "UNCLE!"

CHECK PLEASE

Commando Toilet Training

Let's say you've tried my method for three or four months—just as described—but your child is resisting using the toilet. By this, I don't mean that they're not nailing it every time (that's normal) but that they're refusing to try at all. If you know that they're physically ready but just not cooperating, feel free to give this method a whirl. Note: *this is a second course of action, not a quick fix; there are no shortcuts in child development.*

○ *Set a Deadline:* Tell your child that, in a set number of days, you're going to stop buying diapers, and when you run out that's going to be it. Be reasonable. Give them at least 2–3 weeks of lead-time.

○ *Get Buy-In:* After three or four frustrating months, your child is probably looking for an external deadline to help them over the hump. But you still need their buy-in to make it work smoothly.

   ○ Buy or make a diaper-countdown calendar to use with your child, and have them cross off the date each night before bed. Be sure to count out how many more days are left.

   ○ Take your child underwear shopping and have them pick out underwear they like. Let them wear them around (without pressure) if they want. This means, no getting mad if there's an accident.

   ○ Have your child create a list of times that they can practice using the toilet.

○ *Stick to the Plan:* On the appointed day, toss out any remaining diapers, and let your child know that it's now panty time. Remember, this is your last-ditch effort. If you fold or give in, you're screwed.

○ *Be Ready for Accidents:* This plan, because of its cutthroat nature, is likely to result in more accidents over the short term than any others. Be prepared—buy *lots* of undies, paper towels, and laundry soap. And one of those plastic mattress pads. And some of that carpet-cleaner spray.

○ *Be Kind:* Your child probably has enough shame about this situation. Do everyone a favor and don't add any more. Positive reinforcement here will work a lot better than yelling, screaming, and crying.

6.

It's Only Ketchup
Talking and Listening to Your Kids

THE CORKY CONUNDRUM was Roxy's last straw. It took place during Friday Night Smackdown, my sister's mocking nickname for the evening when her boyfriend's twin girls slept over, thus tripling their household's population of five-year-old blondes. Life with the kids had been rough since Nick moved in, with my niece Amber taking out her feelings of displacement on the twins, and Faye and Lucia responding in kind. As a way of trying to ease the tensions and provide the girls with something to bond over, Roxy had bought a kitten: a rusty tabby they'd named Corky. The girls had agreed to share the cat, and the responsibility of caring for him, but he'd almost immediately become just another thing for them to fight over.

The situation had apparently come to a head that evening, just before Roxy called me. In what was clearly a thinly veiled way of confronting the frustrations of their not-so-blended family, the girls had decided to perform a wedding, in which they planned to marry Corky to Mr. Wonderful, a two-foot-tall talking doll Nick had given my sister for her birthday. When you pulled a string, Mr. Wonderful said things like *"Sure, honey, I'd love to come shopping with you"* and *"No, you don't look at all fat in those jeans."*

"Each of them wanted to be the maid of honor," Roxy said breathlessly between sips of her vodka tonic. "Each of them wanted to be the one to walk them down the aisle, to be the ring bearer, the flower girl, the minister, the best man. But they couldn't agree on a way to choose who would do any of these jobs, and so they ended up in a pile on top of the cat, scratching at each other's faces, and pulling each other's hair. By the time I got into their room, it looked like a scene from a bad women's prison movie."

"So what did you do?"

"That's what I'm getting to here—my *brilliant* solution. You know they all share a bedroom over here, right? So even though I wanted to divide them up, there are no separate spaces to send them to. Instead, I brought Corky into the bathroom with me and locked the door and sat there, plotting my response. It's hard enough being a mom. Being a stepmom is worse, because the stepkids don't really have to listen to you, but you want them to, and you want them to like you, and you want to like them, but you don't want to appear to like them more than your own child. Anyway, I wanted to think of something perfect to say, something that would make me seem like I was in charge but also fair and loving. But by the time I got back to the girls' room, they were arguing again, replaying the entire Corky fight from the beginning. So instead of delivering whatever my brilliant line was going to be, I stood in the doorway, put a hand on my hip, and shouted, 'Okay, new rule. No one is allowed to touch the cat *ever again!*'"

I sighed meekly.

"I know. I didn't even want the stupid cat. I got it for *them.* And if they can't touch it, how are they supposed to take care of it—not that they do anyway. Shit." I could hear my sister light a cigarette. "Why do I say things like that? It's a fucking pet. What's the point if they're not allowed to *pet* it?"

"Don't beat yourself up, Rox," I said. "Parents say things they don't mean all the time."

"No duh. My question is, How do I train myself to *not* do that?"

I sensed that this question wasn't only rhetorical, that my sister was actually struggling with this issue, so I attempted a response. "I suppose the first step is figuring out what you do that doesn't work and seeing if any of those things fall into a pattern."

"I feel like *nothing* I do works. What are some of the big patterns?"

"Well, 'never-ever' statements, like what you did with Corky, are an obvious one to avoid, since they're unenforceable and just set everyone up to break them."

"Great, that's easy. I'll never-ever do that again." Roxy chuckled. "What else?"

I hated being put on the spot like this; it always made me go totally blank. But after a series of difficult and destructive relationships—including Amber's dad, an alcoholic co-worker, and an architect on whom she had to take out a restraining order—my sister had finally found a soul mate in Nick, and I could tell she wanted to do right by him and his girls. I pushed through the blank spot in my brain and searched for answers. "Um . . . you should definitely avoid lying and giving misinformation."

"That's pretty obvious, isn't it? Why would you lie to your kid?"

"I don't know. It seems like parents often do it to get past a problem quickly." Tal's family creed was founded on just such suppressive and needless white lies, so a few good examples starring his sister Lizzie came readily to mind. Since Roxy and I shared a prurient love of watching other people fuck up, I decided to tell them to her in detail.

The first one happened when we were down at Tal's folks' place one Christmas. Lizzie's daughter Violet was around two at the time and had somehow developed an appetite for ice. We were all in the living room having a drink, and since Lizzie's bourbon on the rocks was tantalizingly loaded with ice and readily within the girl's reach on the coffee table, it was only a matter of time before Violet made a move for it. Lizzie yanked the glass away, clearly not wanting her toddler to take a ride on the Wild Turkey. But instead of simply explaining that alcohol was unsafe for kids or that drinking it might make her sick, she pointed a finger at the glass and said, "Hot!"

Violet stared back befuddled, and I could almost see the wheels turning in her mind, wondering why a *hot* drink would have so much delicious ice floating in it. I must have made a face as well, because Lizzie launched into an explanation. After a bad burn and a couple dramatic near misses, she and her husband, Ace, had finally succeeded in teaching the girl that the stove was *hot*. Following this success, they were now using the term as a prohibition against all household dangers. I found this practice to be back-assed at best, but since I was famous for "ruining Christmas" with my snarky remarks, I stayed mum. Of course, Violet didn't buy her mom's bogus lesson either, and as soon as Lizzie put the glass down, she reached for the ice again. Lizzie snatched the drink back and looked sternly at the girl. Clearly shamed by the folly of her previous tactic, she tried a new one. "Poison!" she said, an admonishment that was instantly undermined as she hoisted the cup and took a big gulp.

My sister broke into hysterics. "She says *poison*. Then she *drinks* it."

"I know. But wait, I have another Lizzie story that's even better."

Later that winter, a friend of Lizzie's moved onto her block in Richmond and immediately had her kitchen redone. Since there's apparently some southern badge of honor in being the first to see a new renovation, Lizzie insisted on coming over as soon as the appliances were installed. None of the finish work had been completed, and her friend's cabinet doors were still boxed up alongside her flatware and utensils. Wanting to study the fancy glass-tiled backsplash, Lizzie passed Violet some markers and told her to entertain herself by drawing on the boxes, but as soon as she turned away, the girl pried her way into the nearest one, grabbed a fancy knife, and sliced open her finger.

The cut wasn't particularly deep, but it was a bleeder, and though Violet wasn't squeamish, neither was she exactly comforted by the scarlet fountain shooting out of her hand. Yet instead of reassuring her daughter, and/or using this moment to teach her about the dangers of playing with sharp objects, Lizzie grabbed some shop towels and wrapped them around the cut. "Don't worry," she told the girl, "it's only ketchup."

My sister went silent. "Now that's just plain weird." I heard her rattle the ice in her glass, a tic that meant she was thinking. "But I'm sure I do things like that all the time. In fact, just today, when I picked Amber up at school, she asked me if we could go to the Dairy Bar for ice cream. And because I didn't feel like stopping *or* telling her no, I said the store was closed. When we drove by, she could clearly see that it wasn't."

"Which just diminishes your credibility and authority and makes your kid unsure when—or whether—to ever believe you. Clearly not the best position to be in as a mother."

"Right . . ." Roxy paused.

"What?"

"I just thought of another one. Shit. During the whole Corky thing tonight, as a way of coming up with a 'solution,' I was honestly thinking that I could give the cat away and then just tell the girls that he ran into the street and died."

"Um . . . that's sort of severe. Well, at least you didn't do it."

"I guess. But the worst part is that I didn't just want to solve the problem. I wanted to tell them something that would also make them sad. That's so mean! God," she said, "I'm a terrible mother. Worse, I'm a wicked stepmother, aren't I? Aren't I?"

I nodded. "Yes, dear, you are."

"Okay. So no *never-ever* statements and no lying," Roxy said. "What's one more big one—an easy one—I can use to make these little bitches listen?"

"No *no*'s."

"No-no's, like uh-uh, like 'shame on you'? Or *know*s, like 'know-it-all' or 'mother knows best'?"

"Neither. Just no. The word *no*. Being negative. Especially in terms of directives: orders, commands, things like that." I explained that because negating decrees are censorious and limiting, and thus oppositional to the positive and expansive essence of early childhood, kids quickly learn to tune them out. I also explained that they can be ineffective because they try to stop kids from doing something without providing instructive options. As a way of illustrating this, I gave my sister an example.

"Imagine the girls were playing outside, and when you came out you caught them yanking all the blossoms off your bougainvillea. If you just say, 'Don't pull those flowers off,' and expect an immediate reaction, it's likely that it won't work. This is because you're failing to provide for young kids' cognitive needs. They require reasoning, as well as time to make change and options for redirection. To provide these things, can use what I call the EAR method."

"The *ear* method?" Roxy asked.

By providing your child with rules for how you *do* want them to behave, instead of admonishments for how you *don't,* you give them a template they can use to please you—as opposed to a list of things that they know will get your goat. Still, having to go through this whole three-step rigamarole every time your child does something you don't like can seem like a total pain in the ass. So you can just use PR, or Positive Redirection. Instead of giving them a negative *don't* demand, you tell your child what you *do* want to have happen, and leave the rest of the decision making up to them. "Don't pull off

CHECK, PLEASE

YOUR HANDY GUG CHECKLIST FOR:

Issuing Directives

The EAR method is a stern but constructive communication system. Whereas saying "no" is akin to a military offensive, the EAR method is more like diplomacy. It has three parts:

○ **Explain:** Let your child know how their action/behavior is inappropriate or problematic.

○ **Adjust:** Allow time and reasoning to help your child incorporate your instruction.

○ **Redirect:** Provide guidance about a new, unobjectionable activity or behavior.

Let's say you find your kid yanking all the flowers off your begonia.

○ **Explain:** "The plant needs its flowers to grow."

○ **Adjust:** "I know that picking stuff off plants is fun."

○ **Redirect:** "You can pick *and* help the plants by pulling off their *dead leaves.*"

the flowers" becomes "The flowers need to stay on the plant." "Don't splash in the bath" becomes "The water needs to stay in the tub." You can even distill it down further. If your child is standing on their chair, say, "The chair is for sitting." If they're hitting their sister with a block, say, "Blocks are for building." If they're plucking all the live flowers off your bougainvillea, say, "Flowers are for looking at."

"So," Roxy said, " 'Stop fighting over the cat' becomes 'You need to share the cat.' "

"Exactly."

"Or you could say, 'The cat is for petting.' "

"You could. If you don't have a rule against petting the cat."

"Dickhead," she said. " 'You need to share the cat.' That sounds so much nicer."

"That's the idea."

My sister paused. "That's a total mind-fuck. It turns my whole way of talking to kids on its head."

"Not the *whole* way. You can still make fun of them without their realizing you're doing it. And you can still spell out things you don't want them to understand."

"I guess." Roxy paused again. ". . . I think I'm going to miss the word *no.*"

I smiled. "Trust me, it's overrated."

I heard some mayhem in the background and then Nick's stern voice in response, and I was glad that Roxy and I had had this conversation now, in the early part of this, her first happy relationship. But when I thought about my sister's history, I couldn't imagine her having been open to making these kinds of changes earlier, during her miserable marriage to her ex-husband. And this made me realize how much of parents' ability to be positive with their kids is linked to their own personal sense of satisfaction. I thought to say something about this to Roxy, but I couldn't think of a way to do so that didn't seem patronizing or critical. Fortunately, she rescued me with another question.

"One more thing," she said, "and then it seems like I'm going to have to get back to the zoo. What if I try all this and I don't get it right? Is it like antibiotics, where it's worse if you only take part of the bottle than it is if you don't take any of the pills at all?"

"There's very little that's like that with kids. Besides antibiotics. Kids learn incrementally, so they rarely get something on the first try—think about how long it takes them to get a basic concept like putting on pants. Plus they're totally adaptable. So don't feel pressured to be perfect right out of the gate. You always have more chances."

By way of example, I told her one last story about talking to kids. My first year teaching, I became close with a goofy little African American girl in my class named Sharri. She was usually the last kid to be picked up from the extended-day program I ran, and so we spent a lot of time together one on one: reading books, making projects, or sometimes just talking. She always insisted on being my partner on trips and on sitting next to me during story time, and she always wanted me to rub her back before her nap. She was funny and clever and had a sharp way of summing things up, and I enjoyed the vibrancy of our connection. Then one day, she suddenly became cold toward me. It was like a switch had gone off, and I found it distressing. I figured something might be happening at home, but not yet being very skilled at bridging the home–school divide, I simply sat back and hoped it would pass. Yet the distance continued, unabated. Finally, one evening after everyone else left, I asked her what was going on. She wouldn't say at first, but eventually she relented. "My mom told me that you don't like girls."

I wasn't at all sure how to respond. I figured the best thing to do would be to get the full story directly from Sharri's mom, but I didn't want to talk to her in front of the girl that evening. So the next afternoon I called the mother at work. Frances sighed once I told her. "I'm so embarrassed," she said. "The other weekend, Sharri said she wanted to marry you. I told her she couldn't, and when she asked why, I didn't want to go through the whole process of explaining about your being . . . gay, so 'He doesn't like girls' was the first thing that came out. I really didn't think she'd take it that way."

I was sympathetic—sexuality is a tough topic to approach with a four-year-old—but I told her that kids' understanding of the world is literal and rule bound, which means they'll apply declarations broadly and in ways you might not anticipate. Because of this, the best way to explain things to them is to be clear-cut, without oversimplifying, because when you oversimplify, you can capture unwanted intentions. "Using a concrete example can help," I said, "because it removes what you're saying from the realm of abstraction."

Frances agreed, and though I had to suffer through a few more days of Sharri's distance, by the end of that week she seemed back to her old self. At pickup time on Friday, I asked Frances how she'd resolved things. "I just told her that you were gay. My husband reminded me that she'd heard the term before. She had this baby-sitter named Randy last summer who once brought his boyfriend over, and they'd talked to her about it, simply saying that they were a couple, like me and Ron. I told her, 'Brett's gay. He has a boyfriend. You know, like Randy and Todd.' She looked at me with her big brown eyes all lit up. 'Randy and Todd?' she said, excitedly. 'Count me in!'"

My sister laughed. "Thanks. That makes me feel better."

I was hoping we could keep talking—we didn't get many chances like this—but then I heard girls screaming and Nick shouting for backup. "What's the problem now!" Roxy called, irritation invading her tone. "I've got to go, B. Thanks for all this. It seems really help-ful. But I swear to god, sometimes I just want to say something that will terrorize them and shock them into submission. Something like 'You're giving me cancer!' or 'You're all going to the orphanage!'"

As I hung up the phone, I realized that there was one more benefit to talking to your kid appropriately, one that Roxy and I hadn't had time to discuss: level-headedness. Much of the time that parents are speaking to their child—directing, redirecting, disciplining—emotionality colors what's being said. This isn't necessarily a prob-lem; emotions are expressive. But I know that in parenting, as in most other situations, heated feelings can skew your perspective and cloud your ability to see beyond the immediate. Having an arsenal of constructive ways of talking to your kid is like having a functional bedtime (or morning or mealtime) routine: it provides a dependable and rational guide for getting to the desired solution. And just like having a routine doesn't preclude the idea of having fun, having a set of useful response templates doesn't mean you have to speak to your child as if you're a computerized bank-by-phone system. You're allowed to (and supposed to) let them know how you feel. But having some practical ways to focus your responses to their actions—particularly tactics that shift the onus for solving problems from you onto them—will make their ceaseless stream of needling and instigation much less likely to result in an emotional eruption on either side. You may have to pause and think about what to say before you say it—I still do. But I think this pause is inherently worthwhile; it gives you time to reflect and to refine your message.

MY SISTER CALLED a couple weeks later, sounding upbeat. She wanted to let me know she'd tried the EAR method during their most recent Friday Night Smackdown. Apparently, the girls had started bickering at dinnertime, calling each other names and flicking macaroni across the table. And though Roxy was pissed, instead of losing her cool and yelling at them, she simply said, "Girls, the pasta is for eating." "They froze and looked at me like I'd decoded their language—the way that Cuban lady did at the dry cleaners down here that time you talked to her in Spanish. Not only did they stop throwing their food, but it felt very empowering."

"That's great," I said. "Right?"

"I suppose. But it weirdly brought up another problem. After the food-fight thing ended, Faye stopped eating her noodles. She was pushing them around on her plate like a Zamboni, and when I asked her what was wrong, she just said, 'I hate pasta.' I looked at her like she was crazy. She loves pasta. It's practically the only thing she eats. So, it made me think: you gave me these clues for how I should talk to the kids, but what about figuring out what they mean when *they* talk to me?"

It was a tough question, but fortunately I had a pat answer ready.

I'd dealt with this issue many times with parents at my school. "I know it's hard to hear kids say that they hate things. But you should know that, nine times out of ten, they don't mean it."

Roxy seemed dubious. "But you've always said that kids are literal."

"They are. But that doesn't mean that they're *linear*, particularly in their emotional responses. They're just starting to understand feelings, and cause and effect, so they have no idea how to properly internalize their reactions or attach these reactions to the proper source. So, when they feel ashamed or embarrassed by their behavior, they often project these feelings outward, frequently onto something nearby. It's like kicking the furniture when you stub your toe. 'Stupid fucking bed.' In addition, they know that saying things like 'I hate,' 'I don't want to,' and 'I don't like' are good ways of eliciting a strong reaction from the adults around them, and these kinds of familiar reactions—even negative ones—are comforting when things aren't going their way. I think if you practice the things we talked about, you'll find that, eventually, the kids will have less cause to lash out, and they'll become more capable of saying what they mean."

"Okay, that's great," she said, sounding distracted. "So, can you do me a favor? Can you type up what you said and e-mail it to me? It would actually even help to see that EAR thing written out."

I sighed. "I hate doing shit like that."

I heard Roxy take a deep breath. "I can see that you're upset that your younger sister is asking you for help again. But you like to write, and you enjoy being bossy, so I'm sure you're going to have a great time doing this for me."

"You're using my own directions to trap me," I said. "That's not fair."

"Mom always said, 'Life isn't fair.'"

YOUR HANDY GUG CHECKLIST FOR:

Translating Kidspeak

Young kids are just developing their emotional intelligence, so what they say doesn't always describe exactly what they feel. For example, if your kid says, 'I hate that babysitter,' it doesn't necessarily mean they don't like Vicky, the girl who's been watching them on Fridays since they were a week old. It can mean "I'm sad that you're leaving" or "I'm cranky because it's my bedtime" or "I'm jealous that you're having alone time with Daddy." Kids don't really know how to deal with their feelings, so they often lash out as a way of reflecting or deflecting their anxiety. How you respond makes all the difference:

○ *Don't Play:* Stop yourself from being hooked into arguments and/or debates around statements you know to be ridiculous or untrue ("I hate pasta"). This is a dead-end game and there is no winning.

○ *Mind Mine:* Think beyond the surface and search for the root cause of your child's dilemma.

○ *Feel Real:* Be empathetic in your responses, without being overly invested. "I understand that you're upset right now, but I know you like Vicky, and I'm sure you're going to have a great time with her." This will help your child understand that their emotions are important to you, while also alerting them to the fact that you're not going to lose your shit every time they respond this way.

○ *Talk Good:* If you talk to your kid in the respectful, age-appropriate ways outlined in this chapter, they'll be much more likely to comprehend what you're saying. But remember: when you speak to your child, you're not only trying to get them to understand *you*, you're actually *giving them the tools they'll be using to communicate for the rest of their lives.* You don't want them to end up a stony mass like your dad or a passive-aggressive narcissist like your mom, right? Behave as if what you say, and how you act, is being studied (because it is!).

How to talk to your kids about:
Everything!

Communicating clearly with your child is one of the most fraught and difficult tasks you'll approach as a parent. To do it effectively, it is important to avoid common pitfalls. Below you will find a guide to the most frequently misused communication strategies, as well as descriptions of why each one sucks and what to do instead, and examples of how to turn it around. Get talking, and good luck!

STRATEGY	NO!	WHY IT SUCKS *WHAT TO DO INSTEAD*	YES!
ENDLESS CHOICES	"What do you want for breakfast today? We have cereal, oatmeal, eggs, waffles, toast, fruit, bacon, or yogurt?"	Kids can't readily compare more than a few like items. Additional choice overwhelms and confuses them. *Limit yourself to two directly stated options.*	"You can have cereal or waffles for breakfast. Which would you like?"
OPEN-ENDED OPTIONS	"Go in your closet and pick out something to wear."	Open-ended options give kids more choice than they can handle. *Proscribe limits on their selections. This eases their decision-making process, and lessens the likelihood that they'll pick something that's unacceptable to you.*	"It's cold out today, so when you get dressed you need to pick out a pair of long pants, a shirt, *and* a sweater."
UNDELIVERABLE OPTIONS	"You don't want to go to the store with me? What do you want to do instead—stay here all alone?"	What if your kid says "yes"? Then what? *Every option you offer should be available, acceptable to you, and capable of being delivered on.*	"I'm going to the store and I need you to come with me. Please go put on your shoes and your jacket."

STRATEGY	NO!	WHY IT SUCKS / WHAT TO DO INSTEAD	YES!
INAPPROPRIATE / UNENFORCEABLE THREATS	"If you don't get ready for bed right now, I'm going to send you to live with your evil uncle."	If you can't or don't follow through on your threats, your word becomes meaningless. And your word is core to successful communication with your child. *Any threats you make should be focused on responding directly to the situation at hand.*	"It's bedtime. If you don't get ready right now, we won't have time to read a story before you go to sleep."
. . . OKAY?	"We're going to go to the doctor's office now, okay?"	What if your kid says *no*? Then what? *You're the grown-up. You don't have to clear every decision with your child, especially if their response has no real bearing on your plan.*	"We're going to the doctor's office in an hour. I'll give you a ten-minute warning so you'll know when you need to start getting ready."
LIES	"We can't go swimming in the lake right now because it's full of poisonous crocodiles."	Only crazy people blame their behavior on imaginary forces. *Take responsibility for your decisions. We all make mistakes, and we can't always get what we want. Expect your child to learn to deal with this.*	"We can't go swimming in the lake because I forgot your water wings at Grandma's. I'm sorry."
NEVER-EVER	"Stop throwing popcorn or we're never coming to the movies ever again."	Obviously, impossible to follow through on. "Never" is a totally abstract concept and thus simultaneously terrifying and meaningless to a kid. *Kids live in the present tense and the proximal. Be clear and stay focused.*	"The popcorn is for eating. If you can't behave appropriately at this movie, we're not going to come see *Shrek 18* when it comes out next week."

STRATEGY	NO!	WHY IT SUCKS *WHAT TO DO INSTEAD*	YES!
"NO" AND "DON'T"	"Don't hang off the bed." "No bouncing in your seat." "Don't put so much pasta in your mouth."	After ten zillion "no's" your kid learns to tune you out. *Teach your child to hear what you want them to do instead of what you don't.*	"Lie down on the bed." "Sit steady in your seat." "Take smaller bites."
NOT "NICE"	"You hit your uncle on the head? That's not nice."	*Nice* is a weak and ill-defined term. Kids need things to be concrete. *If you want your child's behavior to change, be specific about what you don't like and give them direction on how to change it.*	"You hit your uncle on the head? Hitting hurts. If you're upset with him, use words to tell him what you're mad about."
KITCHEN SINK	"Honey, stop asking me questions. I'm on the phone with your dad, and I'm trying to get your brother to take his medicine and then I have to drive him to the doctor and your father just told me that I have to pick up the dry cleaning."	By all means, you should explain yourself to your child. But when talking to kids, less is usually more. *Additional or extraneous information often disrupts the strength of your message. Remember, EAR: explain, adjust, redirect.*	"I can't talk to you right now. I'm on the phone. But I'll be done in a few minutes. Then you can ask me whatever you want."
CAN'T YOU SEE?	"Don't interrupt. Can't you see I'm sitting here having a conversation with your uncle?"	Kids *see* very little besides their own needs. This is how they work, developmentally. *It's important to help them expand this perspective, but do so constructively and with respect.*	"I'm talking with your uncle right now. If you need something from me, you can either say excuse me or you can wait until I'm done."

REPEAT AFTER ME   REPEAT AFTER ME   REPEAT AFTER ME

7.

Pinching for Justice

Discipline

WE WERE THE second golf cart in the caravan—Tal and I; his mother, Sarah; and our four-year-old nieces, Violet and Brooke—following some lengths behind the girls' mothers and my father-in-law. We were returning from our daily trip to the ice cream stand, the one commercial outpost on Crimson Pointe, a "Car-Free / Care-Free Island Community" on which we'd been marooned for five days. A glorified sandbar off the coast of Georgia, the Pointe had been built as a haven for wealthy southern retirees and as such consisted of literally nothing but a golf course and row upon row of clapboard McMansions stilt mounted on the eroding beach. Since Tal and I didn't share this demographic's vision of leisure—Waldorf salad, tanning, Anglo-Saxon genealogy—we'd spent most of the week hiding in our room or biking around looking for shade. The afternoon ice cream run was a highlight, our favorite event before dusk, when we could finally start drinking.

As I steered the cart around one of the obese raccoons that seemed to be the island's only form of wildlife (the sea turtle breeding grounds had been wiped out to create a water feature for the golf course), I heard a tinny squawk from the backseat. Thinking it was just Sarah reacting to vehicle's sharp movement, I ignored it. But this small noise was followed by a louder and higher-pitched one, and then a shriek, and then a pair of conjoined howls, and finally, the now too-familiar sound of my nieces' crying.

The golf cart's backseat faced the rear, and so my mirrors offered no assistance. "Is everything okay back there?" I asked.

"Nothing we can't handle," Sarah replied.

"Waaaaaaah!" Violet wailed.

"Waah-ahh!" Brookie sobbed.

I turned to Tal. "Doesn't sound like it's being handled, does it?"

"I said, I'm on it," Sarah insisted. "Girls," she said. "Stop whining. Now."

Nothing changed. In fact, the whimpering only increased in volume and frequency, until it sounded like a horde of seagulls robbed of a hot-dog bun. "Uncle Brett," Brookie eventually cried. "G-g-g-granny p-p-p-pinched me!"

The cart containing the girls' mothers was two hillcrests ahead, out of sight, and we were at least a mile away from the house, leaving us alone with this predicament. I generally try to avoid getting involved in disciplining my nieces (or my mother-in-law)—it's not my place, and it rarely ends well—but given the audacity of the accusations and the vehemence of the shrieking, I figured it would be kind of fun to step in. Since the first step in proper discipline is to collect the facts, this was where I decided to begin. "Did you say that your grandmother *pinched* you?"

Tal's mom leaned in between us, pointed at Brooke, and uttered the three most defensive words in the English language. "She started it."

One Tiny *GUG* Minute On: Acting Out

In the process of developing, children need to experience and explore. As it happens, much of this behavior does not conform to adult rules. But except for a few sociopathic examples, young kids generally don't "misbehave" because they're inherently evil. Their brains are simply very different from ours. Here is a primer on some of what may be going on with your child when they're "being bad."

Le Monde C'est Moi: Young kids are rooted in the concrete and the present and are developing a sense of self in relation to the external world. They therefore have a difficult time seeing beyond their own desires, understanding, or needs. Hence, a toddler bangs a spoon against a plate in a restaurant because they discover that it makes a noise that is interesting to *them.* Their awareness that other people might be bothered by this is minimal to nonexistent. It is your job to explain this to them and then to redirect them to explore something less socially disruptive (shredding a paper napkin).

Missed Manners: Kids have a limited behavioral repertoire, so when they're confronted with an unfamiliar situation, they frequently revert to base instinctual solutions like grabbing and pulling. Your objective should be to create templates that work in a wide variety of situations—using words, expressing their feelings, asking for help—so that even the unfamiliar feels familiar and solvable.

Look at Me: Your child is used to being the focus of your attention, so when you attend to other things—even seemingly innocuous things like visiting with a friend or talking on the phone—they'll often act out in an effort to return themselves to the center. Kids need to learn to deal with sharing your attention, but to help them do so you have to explain this situation to them—probably at least the first couple hundred times it happens. ("I'm going to answer the phone now. When I'm on the phone, I can't talk to you, but I'll be right here and I can talk to you when I'm done.")

Years of experience has taught me that it takes at least *two* engaged combatants to have any kind of effective fight (see chapter 4), and so by the time things come to blows it's generally unimportant who *started* something. Kids are set off by all sorts of things (see Thanks for Sharing, page 120), but neither instigation nor retaliation is an effective means of resolving an issue, so the assignation of blame doesn't really get us anywhere. Ignoring the fact that this explanation had come from a sixty-seven-year-old woman, I put on my best teacher voice. "I'm not really interested in who started it," I said. "I just want to know what the problem was and what everyone did, so that we can try to solve it in a way that doesn't involve pinching and crying."

It took the rest of the ride home to get the story straight—a mile in a golf cart can last a very long time—but it seemed that the sequence of events was as follows: (1) Brooke had finished her ice-cream cone, and Violet was taunting her with the remnants of hers. (2) Midtaunt, during my raccoon-avoiding maneuver, Violet's cone slipped from her hand and bounced off Brooke's shorts, soiling them, before landing in the road. (3) In retaliation Brooke leaned over and pinched Violet on the leg. (4) Instead of acting as a mediator, Sarah took Violet's side and pinched Brookie back.

Kids in my class always amazed me with their ability to choose a mode of physical attack that fit perfectly with their personality. Homer, who was wiry and walked in a gallop, was a flicker. Rudolpho, who had a nervous temperament, was a nibbler. Candy, who was impatient and had a booming voice, was a pusher. Denton, who had a magical smile but was prone to red-faced fits of rage, was a biter—a real skin breaker. And Sophie, who was secretive and hoarded crackers in her cubby, was a surreptitious pincher—her victims never saw it coming. This seemed to say something about people who pinch: they're devious.

Delivering "Justice"

As adults, we have an ability to see the context that surrounds an event or conflict. But young kids' sense of perspective and their understanding of cause and effect are limited—oriented almost solely around themselves, the proximal, and the present tense. Deprived of a holistic view of things, punishments that may seem "fair" or "just" to us often feel out of left field to them: while you're busy sending them to their room for getting chocolate all over your white linen slipcover, they're still focused on figuring out how their hands got all brown. On top of this, the way "justice" is usually meted out—in biblical, eye-for-an-eye terms—often reinforces and confounds the very behavior we intend to counteract: hit your brother; get a spanking, along with an admonishment never to hit. One can almost see the flutter of question marks floating over your child's head. The objective with young kids and conflict should not be about "justice." It should be about creating and modeling templates for dealing with interpersonal situations, templates through which inappropriate behavior can be avoided in the future. Remember to see the big picture here. Providing punishments for every tedious infraction is much less important than setting an overall course your child can use to deal with dilemmas throughout their life.

True to form, Sarah launched into a conniving monologue, one that seemed intended to both cement her innocence and school the girls on why she'd been compelled to act the way she did. The end-up of this diatribe was a blanket statement: "And that's why it's not right to pinch people."

Tal rolled his eyes as we pulled up the driveway. "So says the pinching Granny."

"That's different." Sarah set her shoulders. "*That* was for justice."

Sarah's righteous reasoning was lost on the girls, but it did achieve one notable effect: it got both of them crying again. I tried to distract them by asking them to help me unpack the cart, but they were still stuck in the conflict and their howling simply worsened. Though the garage was deep beneath the house, that supersensitive maternal hearing must have kicked in, because it was only a matter of moments before Lizzie and Cindy came bounding down the stairs, asking us accusingly what had gone wrong.

Tal's sister and sister-in-law both

wanted their girls to have a close relationship—to be the perfect first cousins neither of them had ever had—and so, during these family vacations they always made a big show of pushing the girls together. The problem was, the mothers secretly loathed one another, and so they each used the girls' behavior as a means to passive-aggressively needle and indict their rival. "Now, Violet, even if your mommy allows you to climb on the furniture like an animal at home, when you're with me you're going to walk on the floor like a human." Or "Oh, Brookie, maybe your mommy still lets you throw toys at your friends, but we stopped doing that when Violet was an infant." So when they came downstairs and found the girls screaming and covered in bruises and ice-cream prints, their faces practically lit up.

"Oh, Brooke/Violet," they said nearly simultaneously. "What did Violet/Brooke do to you this time?"

Horrified at having to witness another round of "justice," I decided to try to take control of the narrative. I'd planned to depict the conflict as something menial and resolved, something that didn't even merit a second glance, but sadly, Sarah beat me to the punch, launching into a detailed description of what had transpired. Notably, she left her own actions out of the equation and gave things an intentionality that they'd theretofore lacked. "Violet threw her ice cream on Brooke's new shorts, and Brookie pinched her."

As I said before, tensions between these mothers ran high, and as this was the fifth day of a vacation that had not gone entirely without incident, this statement was more than enough to catalyze a reaction. One of the major points of rivalry between Cindy and Lizzie revolved around the way they handled discipline. Cindy was more consistent and verbal, though her methods often crossed the line into dunce cap–style humiliation; Lizzie was more hands-off overall but when pushed had a greater tendency toward volatility.

But both liked to make a show of modeling their practices for the other, so without further ado, they hauled their girls off to separate corners of the garage, where Brookie was thrown into a rusty lawn chair for a time-out and Violet was yelled at and given a good swat. This meant that three distinct responses had now been levied against the girls, not one of which I felt was helpful or instructive.

Since it's the more overtly problematic of the "systems" modeled here, I'll start with a critique of corporal punishment. As a rule, I don't think parents should hit their kids—and not only because I prefer a fair fight. The goal of discipline for young kids is to help them locate their center and to figure out ways to appropriately deal with their reactions and emotions. Spanking your child demonstrates your own inability to center yourself: it shows you losing your cool and lashing out. In addition, it exerts control solely from the outside, doing nothing to help a child learn how to take on this responsibility. Spanking may be effective in the short term—it clearly communicates your fury, and it may shock your child into stopping a particular behavior—but in the long term, it is a highly counterproductive method. I could always tell which kids in my class were spanked at home: they were the ones who had the hardest time regulating their own behavior; they were always waiting for control to be placed upon them externally.

This doesn't mean I don't sympathize if you lose your cool and end up smacking your kid a few times during the course of their life, especially if they really deserve it. We all reach our breaking point once in a while. When our friend Kate confessed her shame at having spanked her son Max—she'd caught him beating his little sister's head against the kitchen floor—I didn't shun her. "It happens to the best of us," I said. After a moment, I added a confession of my own. "I once hit a boy in my class."

It was Tomaso, a volatile Brazilian kid who tantrummed so violently that he had to be physically restrained to keep him from hurting himself or others (see chapter 8). At some point during one of these outbursts, he'd gotten free of my hold and started pounding on my face, arms, and chest. He was hurting me, and working himself into a dangerous frenzy, but I couldn't seem to get a good grip on him. In desperation, I smacked him on the thigh—not hard, but hard enough to make him pause. It gave me time to grab him and bring him in tight, getting the situation back under control. But while there are many things I've forgotten from my years as a teacher, I'll never forget the look Tommi gave me at that moment. It was a brief but profoundly incredulous stare, as though he'd been robbed of his faith in me.

But enough about spanking! Let's turn our attention back to the garage, where our other niece, Brookie, was being inappropriately disciplined as well: forced to sit in silence while her mother glowered at her. While I've never been in favor of hitting, I will admit to having been a past fan of the time-out. There was a long stretch of time when time-outs were one of the most consistently used items in my disciplinary toolbox. I still believe they can have an effective place, but the way they're implemented generally reflects a devolution and debasement of their intent.

Time-outs are meant to be a transitional step: a place and time for a child to find their center so they can talk about what went wrong and how it could have been resolved differently. They are meant to be a means to an end. But in practice, probably more than 90 percent of the time, I see time-outs being used as a blanket form of punishment—an end in and of themselves—wherein when a kid does something "bad," they get a time-out. I know this firsthand, because this very practice crept into my classroom. When I look back on what I like to call the Winter of Discontent, the core causes seem simple: we had a number of very active and quick-tempered kids in the group that year, and we suffered a particularly brutal November, preventing us from being able to run off their extra energy. It was a perfect storm—add equal parts crazy and stir-crazy, then stir—and the number of infractions of the core classroom rules (use words, respect each other, share, etc.) hit epidemic proportions. In response, I found myself losing focus, and instead of using time-outs as a brief holding place or last resort, I began assigning them more often and more loosely. I found myself sending kids to the time-out chair and forgetting what they'd done. I found myself sending kids to the time-out chair and forgetting about the kid entirely. I found kids beginning to expect, desire, or demand time-outs. One troublesome but adorable boy named Ari even started calling the time-out chair *his* chair, and he'd often sit there, unprompted, as a way of trying to get my attention. I sometimes fell into his trap and got riled up. In what I can only describe as a Foucauldian twist, I once even found myself giving Ari a time-out for sitting in the time-out chair too many times without having been given an official time-out.

Because of all this, time-outs became a marker instead of a tool— a scarlet TO stamped the foreheads of the transgressors—and the kids began to collect or avoid them the way they collect or avoid other exemplars of naughtiness, like being grounded or sent to the principal's office. They even started reporting on the day's time-outs at lunchtime, like junior Walter Winchells making or breaking reputations. "Keenan got two for hitting; he's bad." "Justine got one for throwing food; she's naughty." "Marvis got one for yelling; that's not okay." "Sam didn't get any; he's good." It was horrifying. Time-outs had become a badge for the "naughty" and a symbol of purity for the "clean," neither of which were true or in the service of my goals.

As you know, I believe it's never too late to change bad habits, so during the next staff meeting I announced that we'd be revising our disciplinary policy. Except in the most extreme cases—where kids were out of control, tantrumming, or otherwise needed to be removed from the group—we would do away with time-outs. Instead, we would deal with all problems and transgressions as they came up. Following each conflict, we'd get the participants together, talk through what had happened, and then elicit and model relevant tools for resolution. We'd even have the kids practice using these tools right then: speaking out their feelings and needs, insisting that their friends listen to their words, asking their friends to use words in response, trying to create compromise, and so on. Since kids need to feel supported and as though they have recourse, we also made it clear that whenever they were having trouble figuring things out on their own, they could always ask a grown-up to step in and help mediate.

Having to involve ourselves directly in every little incident—every bump, every grab, every slight or exclusion—made the teachers realize how dependent we'd become on time-outs to superficially quash these issues. It also created a lot of extra work. But as studies in prisons have clearly shown, rehabilitation—through education, anger management, and the provision of real options and opportunities—is a much more effective strategy for reducing recidivism than simply locking people up. It took a while for the effects to show themselves, but after about six weeks or so, things began to change. The weather didn't let up, and we were still trapped inside, but the tenor of the classroom started to shift and the mood became notably calmer. Kids still sometimes had to be separated from a particular material or peer. But by providing clear limits, modeling pathways for solutions, and doing away with the reactive and external imposition of punishment, we placed the responsibility on the kids to come up with their own sense of balance. And since kids generally strive to meet the expectations of the grown-ups around them, it actually worked.

Of course, it wasn't always effective, especially on the first try. For example, one morning, Kirk and Aliah were playing together with the LEGOs when a problem erupted: they both wanted *all* of the yellow blocks. At first, it seemed like they might work it out on their own. But in striving for control, Kirk pushed Aliah, toppling her over as if rushed by a wave. She was fine, but while she was righting herself Kirk grabbed her yellow bricks. Since he wouldn't give them back, she called me over to help. Following protocol, I had them lay out the situation, and when they finished I asked Kirk to think of other methods that he could have used to achieve his goals, *besides pushing Aliah*. Kirk screwed his mouth over to one side and squinted—a look that meant, I'm thinking. Finally, he glanced up at me and shrugged. "Pushed her harder . . . ?"

Again, back to the garage! Having exhausted their useless punishment regimens, Cindy and Lizzie began ushering their daughters inside. The girls were clearly physically and emotionally worn out, and so they were crawling up the stairs in that exaggeratedly lethargic way kids have of moving after a big cry. Tal wanted to retreat and sneak in through the back porch, but I insisted on watching—for prurience's sake but also because I thought my presence might exert a calming influence. I was wrong. Homing in on the sluggish rate at which her daughter was ascending, Lizzie almost immediately began goading the girl.

"Violet!" she said sharply. "Hurry up and get up those stairs."

"But I'm ti-i-i-red," Violet whined.

"I don't care what you are." Lizzie pointed. "Get up and get moving, right now."

Violet paused and looked down. "But Mom-my!"

"Mommy, nothing." Lizzie crossed her arms, steeling her expression, and began counting backward. "Three . . . Two . . ."

The dreaded backward countdown. I rolled my eyes. Could it get any worse?

Violet seemed titillated by what might happen next, but she didn't speed her progress up the stairs, and when Lizzie reached zero, neither was there any end reaction. This wasn't really surprising; none had been promised.

In the meantime, having been granted a reprieve by this roadblock, Brooke had taken out her Polly Pocket! Electrolysis Salon and was playing with it quietly on the step in front of her. Her mother didn't notice right away, but as soon as she did, her anger spiked. (Nothing aggravates a parent more than a child retreating into contentment before the parent is prepared to release their anger.) Seemingly viewing this as another opportunity to play dueling disciplinarians, Cindy began calling to Brooke from the bottom of the stairs. "Brookie Marsha! Move!"

"But Violet's in the way."

"I'm not interested in whether or not your cousin has been taught how to listen. I'm interested in whether or not *you* can listen. Now get up those stairs before I really get mad."

She put a hand on her hip, and I could tell another worthless tactic was coming. I guessed . . . might

CHECK, PLEASE

YOUR HANDY GUG CHECKLIST FOR:

The Countdown

It's important to alert your kids to your expectations and to provide them with a clear picture of what is to happen next, so I'm fully in favor of giving time-based warnings, especially in the lead-up to a transition. But you're not helping anyone, or teaching any lessons, when you start a countdown without rationale, guidelines, or goals. For your countdown to be effective, it needs to meet the following criteria:

○ You've defined its duration.

○ You're counting down toward a *specific* and *explicitly stated* end.

○ This end has an either/or statement attached (either *you* will do X or *I* will do Y).

○ You're willing and able to follow through on this statement when the countdown is complete.

Let's say your child is goofing around while getting into the car. An effective countdown would be: "I'm going to count to five, and by the time I get there you either need to be sitting in your car seat or I'm going to put you in it myself."

Making Threats

There is no disciplinary value to making threats, unless you can and do follow through on them. If you threaten and don't follow through, you have shown your child that you don't mean what you say. This deflates your kid's trust in you, diminishes their capacity to learn clear lessons about limits, and undermines your ability to have your dictates taken seriously. This is particularly true if you initiate a threat *on which you cannot possibly make good* (see chapter 6). If you do this, you communicate to your child that your admonitions are just for show, and/or to instill a momentary sense of fear. Your kid will quickly realize that there is no power behind your words, subverting your authority and rendering your disciplinary practices as meaningless as a warning from the French army.

it be . . . the Empty Threat? Cindy didn't disappoint. She pointed at her daughter. "Brooke. Get up those stairs this minute, or I'm going to lock you in your room, and, I swear, you're going to stay in there for the rest of this vacation."

Apparently accustomed to all this empty bluster, neither of the girls paid their mothers any mind. This enraged the women further and they both bounded up the stairs, grabbed their daughters, and swooped them into their rooms. We heard the slamming of doors, the sounds of muffled shouts, the blare of machine-gun fire (just kidding), and then the now-familiar ring of cries and tears.

Cleared of the blockade, Tal and I walked upstairs and into the kitchen, where I immediately opened us each a beer. "All that crying," I said, "over spilt milk."

"Spilt ice cream," he noted. "But it's in the dairy family."

We took our beers out onto the porch, where we found Sarah in a rocker, reading some upper-middlebrow historical novel. She seemed blissfully ignorant of what had transpired, but she must have heard our musings on the subject, because she set down her book and nodded. "They let it spiral out of control."

Though I was peeved with her—for inciting the girls, for avoiding responsibility, and for escaping from her central role in the ensuing conflict—I had to agree with this assessment. I realize how upsetting it can be when your child disappoints, sabotages, ignores, or annoys you, but the fact that it was so easy for this trivial conflict to snowball into the realm of full-on bedlam speaks to the importance of implementing a consistent and functional disciplinary system: one that can be drawn on in any situation, one that helps all the participants solve for the core problem instead of the symptoms, one that is proactive and not simply reactive or overreactive, and one that allows everyone to release their emotions and move on. This last bit is of particular importance. Your limits have to be clear and enforceable; however, as with allowing a scab to heal, a large part of quality discipline is about knowing when to stop picking.

Wanting some alone time, Tal and I brought our beers down to the beach and sat there watching the shorebirds hunt futilely for the now-extinct species of local shellfish. After about ten minutes, we heard someone coming down the dune path, carrying an ice-laden drink and a rattling folding chair.

Lizzie came into view and plunked down next to us. "Violet fell asleep," she said.

Tal nodded. "It's been a long day."

"Right." She gestured back toward the house. "Sorry . . . about all that."

I shrugged. "No need to apologize. To me at least."

Lizzie sighed. "I know. I have to get my shit in check and learn how to stay calm. Part of the problem is that I get into it with Cindy, and I can't release. But I think half, or more, of it is that I want everyone to see what a great kid Violet is, so when she does anything negative, I rail against it. And instead of supporting her, I get defensive and go on the attack. I just really want everyone to like her."

I put my hand over Lizzie's. "We *already* like her. But she's just a kid and . . ."

". . . I know," she interrupted, "and I can't expect her to behave all the time."

"Right." I said. "That's definitely true. But what I was going to say is, you can't expect us, or you, to *like* her all the time. Good discipline is about creating a system that lets you deal with her effectively even when you don't."

Lizzie smiled, flummoxed. "I've never been much good at systems."

"You're a scientist," I said. "Isn't that all about formulas and equations?"

"Not really. It's mostly about guesswork and going with your instinct. Those systems are what you fall back on when your instincts are wrong."

"Working against instinct." I nodded. "That's exactly what good discipline is like."

GUG'S *TIPS FOR HANDLING:*

Discipline

When confronted with problem behavior, a parent's impulse is often to use any means necessary to make it stop *right away*. This is what I call the Cough Syrup method: it may serve to suppress the visible symptoms but does little to address the underlying causes, often allowing the virus to remain, spread, or recur. The ultimate goal of discipline is to help kids find their center and internalize some basic rules and practices so they can figure out appropriate solutions to problems on their own. Therefore, what you want is something more akin to a vaccine. What follows is a plan of effective short-term processes that when implemented—and given regular boosters—will yield useful long-term benefits.

- *Set Your Expectations:* Kids often aren't aware of what their behavior should be like, even in seemingly familiar situations. Laying things out in advance ("We're taking the LEGOS out for you *and* your sister to use") lets them know what the boundaries are. It also gives you something concrete to refer to if/when they cross the line.

- *Stay Positive:* Kids have a much easier time behaving when you tell them what you *do* want them to do than when you tell them what you *don't*. That way, you're guiding them on how to please you rather than on how to push your buttons (see chapter 6). Instead of saying "Don't grab the LEGOS from your sister," try "You need to share the LEGOS with your sister."

- *Give Peace a Chance:* Kids need experience and reinforcement in order to learn, so don't jump down their throats on the first transgression. It's best to state and restate your expectations and then give them a few chances to follow through before delivering justice ("I told you that you need to share the LEGOS. If you grab them from your sister again, you're going to have to find something else to play with").

- *Find a Focused Fit:* Keep your responses connected directly to the issue at hand ("If you grab the LEGOs, you're going to lose your chance to use them"). This will make it easier for you to choose appropriate reactions and will also keep you from blowing up over minor infractions or making idle or unenforceable threats.

- *Be Brief:* Kids can only understand one cause-and-effect statement at a time—more than that just muddles the issue—so keep your expectations and explanations concise: "If this, then that." Period.

- *Echo:* To ensure that your child understands what's at stake, check that they comprehended what you said. Just asking "Do you understand?" isn't enough. Say, "What will happen if you grab the LEGOs from her again?" then wait for the proper response. This way, you're sure everyone's on the same page.

- *Follow Through:* Like AA, discipline only works if you work it. If you don't follow through, you're undermining your authority and confusing your child. Remember, *if you show your kid that you mean what you say, they'll have less need to test you and will be more likely to adhere to your expectations.*

- *Let's (Not) Get Physical:* The goal of good discipline is to help your child learn self-control. Hitting models your *losing* self-control and over time creates the assumption that limits will always be imposed externally instead of developing internally. Save your backhand for the tennis court.

- *Solve for X:* After justice has been delivered and everyone's had a cooldown period, revisit what happened, and ask your child to come up with a more appropriate response. Note: if this practice is to be effective, it has to be sincere; it can't be a time for gloating, needling, inciting, or criticizing.

- *Move On:* Kids learn by trial and error, so for all this to work, you have to be forgiving about the *error* part. If you hold a grudge, you risk creating a self-fueling spiral where you're constantly seeking examples of your child's negative behaviors, and they're more than happy to oblige. The Fifth Amendment prohibits double jeopardy. Once they've done their time, the slate should be wiped clean.

SAY "UNCLE!"

8.
Pouring Water on a Grease Fire

Tantrums

IT STARTED AS an ordinary morning at the lake. Tal and I were hiding out, half-asleep, in a bedroom upstairs, while downstairs, our friend Danika was being tag-teamed by her daughters—Erica, age five, and Anna, age three. We loved both of these kids dearly, and looked forward to seeing them during what had become a summer tradition: a rendezvous at Danika's place in Chicago, followed by a weekend at her family's summerhouse in northern Michigan. The house had a cupola from which you could see Saugatuck—a formerly picturesque lakeside village, now overrun by fudge shops and midwestern queers—but it sat outside of town on twelve densely wooded acres. Accessible only by a long private drive, and cluttered with enough beds, chairs, and place settings for thirty-five people, it felt like the unkempt clubhouse for some secret society—which is exactly what it had been for Danika's great-aunt and her bohemian friends when they'd purchased it collectively in the 1950s.

Danika's girls were in a combative stage—Erica was unhappy at Anna's recent emergence from babyhood and resultant incursion on what had formerly been *her* "big girl" space—and had spent much of the previous mornings arguing, but it had been comparatively mild downstairs so far, at least as far as we could tell from our perch. We'd only been awakened by three or four outbursts, mostly shrieks from Anna as Erica swiped her favorite toy: a plastic simulacrum of a baked chicken. "Give me back *dinner!*" we heard her scream each time, using the moniker she'd given the poultry, a gift from Danika's mom, Ronnie, who rounded out our crew.

In our years of visiting with friends and relatives with kids—both as hosts and as guests—Tal and I had developed an exacting morning routine that we stuck to with unwavering fidelity: remain in our room with the door shut and the lights off for as long as possible. This protocol served three separate but interrelated purposes. First, it allowed us to sleep off whatever drugs or alcohol we may have ingested the night before, staying up late trying desperately to catch up with our friends or family during the few precious hours that their children were asleep. Second, it prevented us from bearing witness to the kinds of disturbing morning rituals—breakfast on the potty, endless TV viewing, six-year-olds breast-feeding—that might bias us permanently against our parent peers. Finally, it limited the number of waking hours that we had to spend with the kids. Not that we don't love them. But we're childless by choice; we have our limits.

In honing our routine, we'd come to realize that there was a time beyond which it was unacceptable for us to remain sequestered. This magic hour seemed to arrive just before 10:30 a.m., when the coziness of the morning had fully worn itself out, and it was time to start gearing up for other activities. If our appearance was not made before this point, resentment tended to bubble over. During one particularly contentious trip to the ocean with Tal's family, we'd overstayed our alone time and had emerged to an empty house. There was no indication where everyone had gone, and they refused to answer their cell phones when we called. Despite our guilt and shame, we enjoyed the day—reading on the beach, grilling up lunch, having a quickie—but when the crew returned around 3 p.m. they gave us the silent treatment. When they eventually broke down and spoke, we were dismayed to discover that we'd missed out on a junket to the nature center: the island's only attraction. Worse than this, for the remainder of the vacation, we had to endure stage-whispered morning threats from Tal's sister and sister-in-law for their kids to "stop squawking," "quit beating each other with that baton," or "learn how to share that Polly Pocket! Equestrian Center" not because these were appropriate expectations to have of a child but so that they wouldn't "wake the uncles." We had become the scapegoats, the bad cops, the stick behind the carrot, a position that we felt was antithetical to our credo: "avoid conflict and remain adored"

So at around 10:10 a.m., we left the room to face our hosts. The sun had risen over the trees by then, and everyone was out on the side deck enjoying it. Danika and Ronnie were reading celebrity gossip magazines—discussing some starlet's newsworthy "obsession" with a certain yellow tube-top—and the girls were playing together nicely, sharing what appeared to be the host toy for the plastic chicken: an electronic supermarket cash register that would beep and recite the name and price of every ersatz food item they scanned, an act that they found to be inexplicably hilarious. *Beep! Frozen waffles, $3.99. Beep! Canned peaches, $1.29. Beep! Bananas, $2.09.*

"Good morning," we said.

"*Morning?*" Danika squinted. "*We've* been up for four hours."

I shrugged an apology. Luckily, she appeared to have made good use of that time: the girls had eaten, they were wearing their bathing suits under their sundresses, and they'd had their sunscreen applied. We breathed a sigh of relief at this last bit. We'd had to endure sunscreen torture the day before, a hideous process that took so long that by the time it was completed, a storm cloud had blown in, and our beach trip was canceled, resulting in a tedious inside day that revolved around a "double feature"—if one can use this term to describe the act of viewing Barbie starring in *The Nutcracker,* twice.

Hoping to take advantage of the good weather (and good moods), Tal and I quickly enacted sunscreen torture on each other, and when we returned to the deck Erica and Anna were holding hands and joyfully bouncing up and down on a pink foam water raft. Danika wanted to go out front and start packing the car, and since Ronnie was inside searching for something, we offered to stay there and watch the kids.

Things went swimmingly for about the first forty seconds. The girls continued their trampoline act on the raft, to which we added an inane sound track. "Bouncy, bouncy, bouncy; Erica and Anna are bouncy/Bouncy, bouncy, bouncy; on the deck at the beachhousy." Granted, it was only a near rhyme, but they didn't mind. Then, suddenly, in the midst of verse two, Danika reappeared, looking pissed. She put her hand on her hip.

"Erica, get off of that mat right now. We need to put it in the car."

I could just make out the rear end of their Subaru from where I stood and there was still an African termite–sized mound of beach toys waiting to be stuffed in the cargo hold, so why the raft had suddenly become a priority was unclear to me: it looked as if it had been living on the porch for years, faded to the grimy shade of discarded bubble gum; it was far too unwieldy for either of the girls to use safely in the lake; and Tal and I certainly didn't need to be seen on it—it clashed with our suits. Given all our other flotation options, I felt like we probably could have done without it. Erica

Transitions

mediate and thus have very limited capacity
for temporal projection. This means that if
something is happening, they have a hard
time extrapolating to its end, or imagining
where or how whatever happens next will
begin. As adults, we can help them through
these shifts or transitions by providing
explanations, giving notice, and avoiding the
abrupt and arbitrary. (Use the EAR method:
explain, adjust, redirect [see chapter 6]). But
because transitions hold the potential for conflict, they should also be carefully planned
for and made as rarely as possible. For
example, a trip home from school should
not include a sudden stop at your child's
best friend's house to pick up a casserole
dish you lent the kid's mother. Your child will
see this not as a quick layover but rather as
a discrete occasion—and a chance to visit
and play.

clearly shared my opinion and squinted at her mother confoundedly. I appreciated this gesture. But then she allowed a snide addition to leak out—curling her lip and sneering—an addendum that her mother, predictably, did not take to.

Parents' reactions to their kids' behavior often work something like the mythic butterfly effect, where the force of an insect flapping its wings in China compounds with myriad other factors and repercussions to form a hurricane off the coast of Chile. In this case, Erica's actions didn't change the weather, but her simple gesture executed one calm summer morning set off a chain reaction involving literally hundreds of variables—pride, stubbornness, sleep deprivation, skin irritation—to create a perfect storm all its own. Even the most sophisticated computer models couldn't predict precisely what caused Danika's decision, but instead of forgiving or ignoring her daughter's transgression, she was propelled toward confrontation. "Erica," she said, lurching slowly toward the girl like some sort of Japanese movie monster. "Get. Off."

At this moment, I realized two things. First, we weren't going to make it to the beach that day. Second, life was probably about to get very ugly.

By not attending to her kids' need for help with this transition,

Danika was inadvertently priming the pump for a conflict. I'd seen this effect many times before, particularly at pickup time at my school. A child would be engaged in an activity and a parent would show up and immediately try to whisk them away, insisting that they get their coat on *right that second* or give up their tea party and fetch their backpack *at once*. Meltdowns and screaming fits would inevitably ensue. Now, I know that parents face many irksome temporal pressures that I don't—battling the afternoon rush hour to drop their child off at bassoon lessons, preparing meals that are served in something other than a shot glass, reading *Olivia* seventy times each night before bed—but building in just thirty seconds of buffer time around any major shift in location or action doesn't seem like it should make or break the daily routine. Plus, if you don't slot in a bit of space for transitions on the front end, the results on the back end tend be much more time consuming—and irritating.

Though the situation clearly conformed to this problematic pattern, Danika dove into it, literally head first. Her face transformed into a seething mask, she lunged at her daughter's feet and began determinedly pulling at the raft. "This isn't going to end well," Tal whispered, turning away. I nodded and joined him in averting my gaze, but not only because of the predictable nature of the outcome. I'd seen these devolutions many times before, and for me the worst part isn't observing the result but watching the lead-up. There's the adult's expression as they lock themselves in for battle with their kid: a look of unbridled rage, suggesting the kind of superhuman strength that allows a mother to lift a car off a trapped child—but in reverse. Then there's the absurd and obvious disparity in the capabilities of the combatants—brontosaurus versus worm, Muhammad Ali versus Don Knotts—and the contrasting seriousness with which the parent seems to view the challenge. Finally, there's the way in which bystanders are expected to act like none of this is occurring. Seemingly aware of this last fact, Anna stepped aside and began feigning interest in a nearby gum wrapper. But Erica stood her ground, refusing to move, until eventually, Danika yanked hard enough to topple her. Fortunately—and quite comically—she landed on the mat, which broke her fall.

"Get off this raft right now!" Danika yelled.

"I'm bouncing on it!" Erica screamed insistently, still stuck in her last activity, the one before the surprise transition.

"No, you're not."

"Yes, I am."

"No. You're. Not." Danika made a definitive move for the raft. But this last-ditch last-grab seemed to cue some sort of primal response in the girl. And like a viper threatened by a relentless predator, Erica reared back, hunched her shoulders and hissed at her mother, visibly misting her face with spit.

Four things happened simultaneously at this moment. First, Danika leaned in and grabbed Erica's arm, abruptly yanking her off the mat. Second, the intuition that allows grandmothers to always be present at the precise moments in which their daughters are behaving with the greatest disregard for their grandchild's well-being kicked in, and Ronnie reappeared. Third, Tal and I averted our eyes, feeling empathetic for everyone involved. Finally, Erica, having now been robbed of her morning's pleasure, having been uselessly engaged in a battle with the person she loved most in the world, and having been physically mauled, went, as we like to say, *full-on nuclear.*

Having worked with young kids for as long as I have, I've seen more than my share of tantrums. I had a girl named Erin who used to lie on her back on the classroom floor and spin, in a sort of spastic imitation of break dancing, pounding her feet and elbows on the ground and screaming "I'm *really* upset," in a warbling tenor. I had another girl in my class named Popo who used to tantrum silently:

she just sat there with her mouth open, as tears streamed out unceasingly. It was heartbreaking, like a puppy who'd been debarked. I had a boy we called Big Rolf, whose mother was an Amazonian East German model, who used to tantrum so frequently and with such vehemence that we had to create a special area in the classroom to accommodate his fits, complete with piles of pillows and paper that he could punch and shred to release his aggression. And I had a boy named Tomaso (who you heard about in chapter 7) who tantrummed so wildly and with such risk to himself and others—literally upending tables and emptying shelves, like some rampaging husband in a bad Lifetime movie—that I had to be trained in a state-sanctioned technique for restraining him. I would bear-hug him from behind and pull him into my lap, placing him in the V formed by my outstretched legs. I'd then cross my calves tightly over his ankles, wrap his arms across his chest, and secure them with mine like a straitjacket. Then I'd press my chin onto the top of his head firmly enough to prevent him from rearing back or biting me. We often had to remain in this position for as long as fifteen minutes, until he had literally screamed and struggled himself to the point of complete physical exhaustion.

This isn't to say that tantrums can't be funny, particularly when viewed from the outside. I often can't help but laugh at kids falling apart in public places—airports, restaurants, the supermarket checkout line—and I imagine how silly all of my students and I must have looked when someone inevitably lost it during our daily walks to the park or while on one of our adventurous class trips. But, while I think everyone would agree that the hissing was a brilliant flourish, Erica's tantrum was decidedly unamusing. Part of this was because we were supposed to be on vacation. Part of it was because it occurred at the inducement of someone we loved. And part of it was because of the way the girl went about it: each of her shriek sets came on like a fighter jet passing at speed—a swelling crescendo punctuated by an eardrum-rattling sonic boom that was both gut wrenching and wildly intrusive. But what was really unfunny was that in the midst of the tantrum, Danika decided to try to talk to her daughter. "I told you I wanted you to get off the raft. I told you we needed to pack it up. But you wouldn't listen. That's why I had to grab it, and that's why you're crying."

Erica howled louder, her eyes rolling about unfocused like a pair of marbles caught in a centrifuge. But despite her obvious immobilization, Danika continued to upbraid the girl. "Now stop crying, get off that raft, and help me carry it to the car! Stop crying!" She put her hand on her hip. "Now, Erica. Now!"

At this point, the sound of their voices melded into a cacophonous roar, and I nudged Tal and we led Anna inside. We found her plastic chicken and played dinner party in the living room, doing our best to ignore the din. Anna looked panicked, likely thinking she was next, and Tal and I tried to soothe her by affecting inane British accents. "Isn't this the most delicious plastic chicken you've ever eaten?" I asked Tal. "Yes," he answered. "I must say, this is the most delicious plastic chicken I've ever eaten."

The yelling continued unabated until, like an inverted bar brawl, the fight came crashing *inside*. The combatants entered the bedroom—in a cartoonlike whorl of cries and flailing limbs—and after a few more minutes, during which we could literally feel the floor shaking, Danika finally stormed out, panting. Erica's vulturesque squawks could still be heard from within. But just as it sounded like she was running out of steam, Danika shouted, "Stop that whimpering!" and crashed back in for another round.

Since Danika herself seemed to be in a tantrumlike state, I followed my own advice and kept my big mouth shut, and she eventually retreated onto the deck. Erica remained in the bedroom, but

One Tiny *GUG* Minute On: Tantrums

As adults, we're always telling each other how healthy it is to release our emotions. Believe it or not, a real tantrum—the kind where your child is rolling-on-the-floor-screaming—is an example of exactly this type of sharing. Granted, it may be loud and annoying, it may occur at an inopportune and embarrassingly public moment, but it's one of the few tools your young child has for expressing themselves when they're emotionally overwhelmed. In this, a tantrum is as natural and healthy as their need to pee after drinking four juice boxes or to vomit after eating tainted shellfish: it's a way for their body to rid itself of emotional toxins. As always, it's your response to your child's behavior that communicates to them the potential effects of their actions. If every time your child tantrums you go running for something to placate them—a cookie, their favorite toy, a video—they will figure that this is an acceptable means to achieve this end. If every time they tantrum you try to force them to stop screaming, they may develop negative associations with displays of emotion and may be hindered in finding appropriate outlets for their feelings and frustrations.

A tantrum is, by definition, a moment in which your child has exceeded their emotional capacity and is incapable of processing any additional information. So while you may think that speaking to your child or providing an explanation will add a comforting layer of rationality to the situation, trying to calm a tantrumming child by initiating a discussion is like pouring water on a grease fire: it simply causes sputtering and encourages the flames to spread and burn longer. Your goal in dealing with a tantrumming child should therefore be to step back and allow the event to run its course. This doesn't mean you should ever try to induce a tantrum as a way of encouraging them to let off steam—that would be like introducing an invasive species to control some natural pest, and we all know how well that usually works out—but it does mean that *tantrums are not a time for trying to communicate with your child*. Let it burn. There'll be plenty of time for talking later.

Ronnie came in and sat on the floor by Tal and me. She was clearly shaken by what she'd seen, but instead of keeping it to herself she started critiquing Danika's parenting style. I always say that grandmas and grandkids have a special bond—they share a common enemy—but I didn't know how to react to this. Danika had told me horror stories of being raised by Ronnie: never having been given any limits, seeing a stream of stoned grown-ups behave idiotically, suffering through an easily curable case of pinworms for all of first grade.

Luckily, before I needed to respond, the bedroom door opened and Erica emerged. From where she stood she could see out to the porch where her mother had at some point retreated, and into the living room where the rest of us were gathered, and she seemed uncertain which way to go. She eventually decided to join us. Her face was flushed, and there were big red circles around her eyes; she looked like one of those giant stuffed raccoons that you might win at a cheap local carnival. Without smiling or saying a word, she sat in Tal's lap. He offered, and she accepted, a plastic drumstick.

After a moment, I went out on the deck. I was hoping to move on with the day, perhaps even salvage the beach trip. But before I could say anything, Danika put down her magazine and pointed. "Don't even ask me if we're going to the lake. After that little performance, she's not going anywhere."

"You could stay here," I offered. "We'll take Ronnie and the kids."

"Oh, now you're trying to get away from me? You're taking her side?"

"I'm not taking anyone's side," I said, though she'd clearly hit on something—I did feel a need to steer clear of her for a bit. "I thought it might give you a break."

"I don't need a break. Forget it."

I bit my lower lip. I could tell Danika felt embarrassed and backed into a corner by her behavior, and while I wanted to offer her an out

I didn't want to overstep the bounds of Gay Uncledom. "It seems a shame to waste such a beautiful day," I said. "How about we take the girls to that playground in town? We can get them lunch at the diner down there and have them back in time for a nap."

Danika squinted, unconvinced. "Will you bring me back a burger?"

I nodded.

"And a milkshake?"

"Yeah. Of course."

She shrugged. ". . . Fine."

The five of us drove down to the park: Tal, me, Ronnie, and the girls. Erica insisted on bringing Debbie, a beat-up plastic doll that she'd had since she was born but that she'd given up playing with regularly at least a year before. This gave me some indication of how fragile she was feeling.

The playground was sandy and rather dismal, but Tal bowed and opened the gate like it was the entrance to god's kingdom. Ronnie parked herself on a bench and took out the copy of *To the Lighthouse*, which she tried to read every summer. Tal and I walked the girls to the swings. Anna climbed up and Tal started pushing her, but Erica hung back, gently cradling her doll.

"Do you want a push?" I asked.

She shook her head. "I have to take care of Debbie. She's upset."

I knew who was really upset and dealing with caregiving issues, but I nodded understandingly. "Well, I'm pretty good with kids. How about I babysit for Debbie? Then you can go and play on the swing."

Erica considered this for a moment and then gently passed her over. I thought to lay the doll on the bench next to Ronnie but didn't want to risk getting caught up in another critique of Danika. Instead, I plunked her in the sand and started pushing.

We stayed at the playground for nearly an hour. Saugatuck had long been a haven for tacky gay and lesbian couples, but it had recently become a haven for tacky gay and lesbian *families* as well, and as Tal and I pushed the girls we had to endure the smug and presumptuous smiles of homo parents who assumed that we were part of their tribe. Now, I'm not opposed to gay people's right to have kids—everyone is entitled to dig whatever shape grave they like—but I was feeling a bit disdainful of the whole parent–child relationship, so when a butch mom asked me how old Erica was, I just shrugged. "I guess around four or five?" I delighted in the look of horror that came across her face.

After about ten minutes on the swings, some of Erica's trademark goofiness began to reappear, and her face started to fade back toward a more human coloration. So it was fortunate that it wasn't until we were on the deck behind the Burger Barn that the girl realized there was something wrong with Debbie. She was distracted by Tal's gift of her first-ever ice-cream sandwich, but she kept tilting the doll's head back and studying her face, looking increasingly concerned. Finally, I asked her what the problem was.

"Debbie's eyes are broken," she said. "They're supposed to close when you lie her down, but only one is closing, and just partway."

I watched as she demonstrated, laying the filthy doll down on the picnic table. It was true, only one eye was shutting, causing Debbie to look like a drunk passed out on a park bench. As I leaned in for a closer examination, I spotted a few grains of sand clumped in the corner of her eye, almost certainly a result of my own negligence. I made a face. I knew that tantrums were like lightning strikes—or sex after thirty—very unlikely to happen twice in a row. But I still worried that the situation might set Erica off. "I think . . . ," I said tentatively, "that might be my fault."

Erica stared at the doll for another moment, before fixing her attention on the treat in her hand. "I never had an ice-cream sandwich before," she said. "It's like, the cookie is the bread, and the ice cream is the meat."

Erica has never let me forget that I blinded Debbie—she brings it up nearly every time I see her, always with a wry and weary smile—but she allowed it to drop as a topic that afternoon. In fact, the whole rest of the day felt drained of emotionality, as if no one could muster the strength to refill their reserves. So I was nervous later that evening when I spotted Tal coming in from the kitchen, looking panicked. He'd been helping Danika fix dinner, and I worried that he'd somehow riled her up or offended her by challenging her earlier behavior. His news was worse. "We're out of vodka."

I volunteered to drive to town, and Danika offered to come along. We chatted emptily for most of the ride, talking about Ronnie and the weather, until she eventually circled back to the day's events. "I heard you broke Debbie," she said.

"Yeah. Sorry." I shrugged. "I was thinking we might be able to suck the sand out of her with that vacuum they have at the do-it-yourself car wash."

"Good idea." She nodded. "Really, it's fine. I'm just glad that Erica didn't have another fit."

I smiled, nervous about how this conversation might go. I've found that it's often easier to talk to my parent friends about perilous issues like their weight or their intractably petty relationships with their siblings than it is confront their child-rearing practices. I'd learned that telling an elucidatory tale from my days as a teacher was often a way to make my message heard, but that it was best to choose an example that was a standard deviation or two removed from my friend's situation. So as we walked through the aisles of the liquor store, I told Danika the story of Big Rolf's classroom tantrum corner, where we'd let him go and literally punch and shred his heart out. "Leaving a kid alone when they're out of control and letting them work through their emotions really helps to teach them how to find their center."

Danika seemed to consider this for a moment. "That's a great idea," she said, her eyes wild with the hint of deviance that kept us close. "Maybe next time Erica has a tantrum, I can put her in the bedroom with that electronic cash register, and she can beat on that." She smiled broadly. "I hate that fucking thing."

GUG'S TIPS FOR HANDLING:

Tantrums

Tantrums represent a breakdown in your child's ability to deal with their world. But they also serve an important purpose: they purge your kid of their emotional backlog. It's like emptying your bag of all those coins, half-used tubes of lip balm, matchbooks, and receipts: it's not exactly *fun*, but it's certainly better than carting them around with you forever. Here is some advice for responding to these fits.

- *Make a Firebreak:* It may seem counterintuitive, but instead of trying to extinguish your child's tantrum imagine your job as akin to that of firefighters in the national forests: make a firebreak. You can exert control over the tantrum not by trying to put it out but by digging a trench around the flames and giving it a wide berth, thus cutting off its source of additional fuel.

- *Zip It and Zip Out:* During a tantrum, words are fuel, your anger is fuel, even your presence can be fuel. Get the picture? Let your child know that you love them and that you'll be nearby. But don't hover. Back off and give them some space. If you play with fire, trust me, you're going to get burned.

- *Don't Try to Solve for "Causes":* While the flames of a tantrum are burning, your core objective is not to figure out why the fire started; it is to find the most effective way to put it out. It doesn't matter whether it was catalyzed by a misunderstanding, an act of god, or some spilled milk. While it's raging, it must be dealt with, not discussed.

- *Let It Burn Out:* If you step back and let the tantrum run its course, your child will emerge feeling relieved, having burned off all that accumulated dead wood. I'm not saying beautiful flowers will immediately begin to sprout, but nothing can germinate if the underbrush isn't cleared once in a while.

- *Talk Later:* Find a calm moment after the fact—*significantly* after the fact, maybe even the next day—during which you can discuss what occurred and search for useful alternatives. This pause will not only allow your child to attend to what you're saying—liberated from the clouding screen of their own heightened emotions—it will (hopefully) let *you* see the situation from a clear perspective as well.

- *Progress Takes Time:* If you allow kids to tantrum in this way, *over time* they will learn how to work through their emotions and calm themselves down. As with everything in a child's development, this progress will *not* be instantaneous or linear. So be patient. Rome wasn't burnt in a day.

SAY "UNCLE!"

9

Fairy Houses
Friendship

TAL'S SISTER LIZZIE steered us toward the donut shop, which was blessed with the rather repugnant moniker The Sweet Hole. A pit stop here was apparently a privilege she lorded over her daughter Violet on the days she took her to preschool: if the girl got out of the house on time, if she behaved herself for the duration of the walk, if she avoided the sidewalk cracks and the resultant breaking of her mother's back. But a visit was totally guaranteed on this particular morning: Tal and I were accompanying them to our niece's Montessori school, and since it was not yet dawn the Gay Uncles were in desperate need of mega-doses of carbs, sugar, and caffeine.

According to Lizzie and her husband, Ace, Violet had been talking about this outing for weeks. Tal was probably her favorite grown-up on earth, and she wanted to share her entire life with him. Tal was similarly devoted and had a tireless ability to entertain the girl when we were together, spending hours tossing her around in his parents' pool, building oceanfront sand castles until his skin blistered, even enduring full games of the torturous and interminable Chutes and Ladders. I was less enthusiastic about the trip. Besides the fact that I'm a cranky bitch in the morning, I was ambivalent at best about the Montessori philosophy. I felt much the same way about it as I did about Buddhism: I respected its adherents' dedication to their process, but I had absolutely *no* understanding of or interest in its goals. Lizzie was also anxious about our visit, but her concerns were much more personal. She'd laid them out over drinks the night before: she was worried about what we'd make of her daughter's relationship with Marquis.

Marquis, it had become clear during our conversation, was a boy in Violet's class, one she'd been talking about a lot recently: Marquis did this, Marquis did that, Marquis says this, Marquis hates that. It seemed to me that Marquis might be, at the ripe old age of four, our niece's first real friend. Violet was a bright and unique little girl—precocious, outgoing, and, like her scientist parents, wildly interested in the natural world—but she also had a number of peculiar tics. She was extremely linear in her thinking and needy for adult attention, and she was often paralyzed by arcane fears: giant lobsters, falling boulders, ruptures in the time–space continuum. She also had difficulty understanding the "logic" behind typical four-year-old shenanigans like pratfalls, silly noises, and imaginary play, making her standoffish with kids her own age. The end-up of all this was that she hovered impassively on the outskirts of her peer group.

Given all this, I thought that the idea of her developing a friendship would be seen as a positive step. Yet as our cocktail hour progressed, instead of embracing Marquis' role, Lizzie and Ace had variously described him as Violet's swami, her dirty pleasure, and even once as her axis of evil. Ever a booster for the underdog, I eventually felt compelled to ask what was up.

"He's weird," Ace said.

"Weird isn't always bad," Tal offered.

"This kind is." Lizzie nodded. "He's . . . ungrounded. He lives in his own world. Plus, he's sort of *naughty*. He's wild. He doesn't follow directions. He doesn't respond when spoken to. He was once caught trying to drink out of the classroom fishbowl."

I nodded. Their concerns certainly made some sense. Parents often fear the influence of their children's friends, in some cases rightfully so: we all remember those kids who introduced us to vice. And, of course, the onset of peer relationships signals the beginning of the end of parental control. Developmentally speaking, a child's immersion in and identification with the world of their immediate family is greatest at birth and slowly wanes from there in favor of connections with friends. But there seemed to be something else at work for Lizzie and Ace. Like most of the people I knew, they'd been social outcasts in their youth, and while they didn't exactly cultivate Violet's disengagement from her peers, it was something they supported in a variety of subtle ways. They almost seemed to wear the girl's disdain for her cohorts as a badge of honor, as if she'd figured out early how dumb and cruel kids could be. I guessed that the idea that she'd chosen *any* child as a friend—particularly an allegedly rowdy and nonintellectual one—felt, to them, somehow beneath her.

My theory was proven out as we entered the classroom. The rest of the kids were gathered around the water table, but instead of encouraging Violet to join, Lizzie pointed contemptuously at the group. "Look at them all clustered together," she said, glancing at the group of four-year-olds, all happily measuring and dispensing liquids. "Like sheep in a herd, right Violey?" She patted her daughter's head. "Violet's five lessons ahead of all of them." She pointed at a chart that displayed the dates on which each child had completed the requisite curricular tasks. Violet was indeed far above the norm, having plowed her way through basket weaving, lanyard tying, metal forging, and many other tasks Maria Montessori had designed in postwar Italy to help poor rural youth advance the country into the modern era.

What all this meant to twenty-first-century Virginians was beyond me, but I smiled at the chart, studying the class list. This was the South, so instead of the old Jewish names that had become so popular in New York—Max and Sam and Esther and Hannah—the list was full of WASPy titles that evoked the Gilded Age. There were two Tylers, two Landons, two Madisons, and three Emmas. These kids were all clumped up in the middle of the chart. I searched for Marquis. He was easy to find: he was right at the bottom.

"Which one of them is Marquis?" I asked, gesturing toward the water table.

"He's not here yet." Lizzie checked her watch. "He's always late."

As she said this, a petite African American woman with a tremendous hairstyle came pouring through the door. She was wearing a burgundy leather coat, a radiant blue dress, and a pair of killer boots and was carrying what had to be the largest purse I'd ever seen. She waved to the kids at the water table, and a few of them ran over to give her a hug. She reminded me of a fantastic assistant teacher I'd hired at my school, a West Indian girl named Carla, who was attending college full time *and* taking care of her son and her grandma, but who still managed to find time for clubbing and trying to start a clothing line. In fact, she reminded me so much of Carla and was greeted so warmly by the class that I assumed she worked there. So I was startled when she turned back toward the door and called out sharply, "Marquis! Mommy says get in here now."

Marquis peeked around the doorframe and took a few tentative steps in. He looked a lot like his mom but was dressed much more conservatively, in a crisp blue shirt and khakis and a pair of spotless hiking boots, and he was as reserved as she was gregarious, silently hiding behind her leg. She stroked his head and tried to shoo him toward the water table, but he remained stuck. That is, until Violet called his name, at which point he sloughed off his backpack and ran across the room to embrace her.

Marquis' mom followed his action, smiling broadly. After putting his things away, she walked over to us. "You must be Violet's uncles. I've heard *all* about you." She pointed at me and Tal, making her hands into guns, then turned to Lizzie. "You know," she said, "we still owe these two children a playdate."

"I know." Lizzie nodded, watching as Violet and Marquis leapt up and down, huddled together in an enveloping hug. "Let me check with Ace about our schedules."

"Okay. But I think we need to do it soon. As in, *before* they elope . . ."

Marquis' mother called his name and blew a kiss good-bye, and the boy mimed his version of a similar action, but not once during this process did he release Violet.

"That's quite a mommy," I said in her wake.

Lizzie smirked. "Tell me about it. She looks kooky and scattered, but she's managing editor of *Virginia Fine Living*, and she's totally relentless. She's been asking for that playdate since the second day of school. I'd really like to set something up, but Marquis just seems so . . . inappropriate for Violet." She glanced at the two kids, still conjoined and gurgling giddily. "I can't imagine the two of them could entertain each other for a full afternoon."

I'd heard this concern many times before. Parents rightfully want their child to experience maximum joy and are suspicious of any situation that may seem less than optimal. And I've definitely heard tell of get-togethers gone awry—ones that end in a child being bored, bullied, or beaten. But I've found that when parents express reservations about their kid's friendships, the problem is more often rooted in an internal conflict *of their own* rather than anything having to do directly with their child.

These issues frequently grow from the disparity between parents' image of who they believe or want their child to be and what they feel is reflected about their child by the kids they choose to associate with. Our friend Kate often speaks disparagingly about the child her son Max has selected as his best friend: a scrawny and nearly translucent boy named Owen. Not only was she angry that Owen was the youngest and least verbal kid in the class—which made her feel that Max was setting too low a bar—but it irked her that whenever they got together, every activity they engaged in somehow managed to culminate in Max lying facedown on the floor and Owen mounting and dry-humping him. Building with LEGOs: humping. Playing pirates: humping. Baking cookies: humping. While the boys seemed to enjoy this, Kate was concerned about what it meant for Max's future. "I knew he was gay from the day he was born," she said, "but I guess I always kind of hoped he'd at least be a 'top.'"

Lizzie and Ace seemed to be having a similar reaction. While they certainly didn't want Violet to be conventional, they also didn't want her to have to suffer through the derision they'd experienced in their own youth. And though they'd fostered in her a protective armor—a haughty rejection of the whole idea of peer connections—her friendship with Marquis had not only broken this down, but also seemed to signify that she was a weird outlier *just like him.* For all their talk about embracing their daughter's iconoclasm, they clearly didn't want this association.

Pushing your kid to confront and embrace difference isn't only relevant because it's key to their developing sense of self, or because ignorance and intolerance are literally threatening to destroy the earth. It's important because we're an overly individualistic society and are becoming increasingly more so—with bigger gates, houses, lawns, and checkpoints between us—and challenging ourselves to get out of our comfort zones has become progressively more difficult. This has created a spiral of increased segregation not only in terms of class and race but in terms of our ability to resolve interpersonal problems humanely: our first response to everything is to either retreat or call security.

Friendships are the front line in children's battle to learn about human interaction. So while you have little control over the nation's policies for subsidizing the creation of ever more isolated exurbs, or

One Tiny *GUG* Minute On: Temperament, Fits, and Friendships

Kids are born with individual and innate ways of responding to the world. We call this their temperament, and it includes things like how readily they get involved in things, how much stimulus it takes to get them to respond, how intense their reactions are, and how consistent they are in their responses. When these temperaments bump up against each other, as they do in your kid's initial social forays, your child is learning how to interact with others and is forming pathways for the future. These pathways, however, change and grow as your child and their friends change and grow. Thus, while each companion impacts your child's development, it is not the be-all and end-all. It's therefore extremely important not to limit their peer options. Exposure to a variety of personalities not only furthers your child's sense of self but also enhances their concept of what it means to be a human. Don't stick them into an inflexible vision of who you think they should be. Remember how wrong your own parents were about you?

ceding communally owned public lands to extractive indus-
tries, you have total control over the rules that govern your kid's
personal and interpersonal interactions. I strongly recommend the
implementation of tactics that prime the social pump, that
break down barriers, and that encourage wide-ranging exposure.
For example, at my school, on our daily walks to and from the
park, I would intentionally partner up kids who weren't already
friends. I would seat four random kids at a separate lunch table
each day for an intimate dining experience. I would insist on gathering in a circle whenever we had discussions so that we could all
see and listen to each other. I even insisted that if parents were
going to distribute birthday party invitations at the school, then
every member of the class had to be invited.

We all delighted in the unpredictable and evocative pairings that
developed as a result: Rolf, the giant tantrumming East German,
befriending Takashi, a silent sliver of a Japanese boy; Elena, a spastic and chubby girl whose mom was a drug-addled fashion designer,
and Pablo, a meticulous Mexican boy who wanted to be an architect; Hope, a tough Korean jockette, and Albert, a shifty white
kid who loved Frank Sinatra. The list went on and on and was
always morphing and reconstituting as kids grew and learned from
one another. It was as if the classroom's fixed number of members
were constantly changing and recombining to form an endless
series of groupings—sort of like the last season of *Melrose Place*. Shy
Albert became confident and started working with Rolf in the
block area. Bossy Hope began deferring to the increasingly elegant
Elena. Quiet Takashi belted out Oaxacan drinking songs Pablo had
taught him.

Because we wanted kids to develop close one-on-one friendships
as well, we also strongly encouraged parents to host or suggest
playdates: times when kids could get together outside of school.

One Tiny *GUG* Minute On:
Playdates

I've always hated the term *playdate*—it sounds like the name of a courtship ritual for middle-aged divorcées—but I believe strongly in their power. They are milestones for kids, and can be profoundly transformative, catalyzing leaps in socialization, as well as affecting change in other realms. For example:

- *Sharing the Self:* During a playdate, kids are provided with an opportunity to share their space with others. Since a child's home is core to their construction of self, in sharing it, they are sharing key aspects of their identity. These visits also push them to experience and integrate similarities and differences in how people live.

- *Proximal Development:* Playdates allow your child to see how their cohorts accomplish tasks, solve problems, or approach situations. They also provide the opportunity for your child to teach their friends how *they* do things. Both aspects are of key developmental importance, as kids are often better able to integrate information and skills presented by a peer than those presented by an adult.

- *Unifying Realms:* Young kids don't share our understanding of context. For them, the life they live in their own home is often seen as completely separate from the life they live outside, or at school. It's like that Demi Moore movie where she has one existence in contemporary America and then another in her dreams in revolutionary France. Bridging these realms provides kids with the opportunity to test, apply, and internalize the rules from these various worlds, helping them to unify their experiences.

- *Solving Problems:* Parents often fear conflict in playdates, and certainly no one wants to see their kid instigate a pointless argument with a friend over who gets to use the goddamn pink marker. But, for young kids, peer conflicts reflect an opportunity for growth. Kids learn where their needs end and others' begin; they learn how to integrate this knowledge and recognize needs before they become a conflict; and they learn skills and templates for crafting mutually acceptable solutions.

Playdates are meaningful for a variety of reasons, most important because they allow kids to put into practice, in an intimate setting, the various interpersonal skills they've picked up. They're a way of extending knowledge and practicing it in the real world, and as such are necessary for proper development. They don't *need* to happen until kids are ready (for most, around age three), but I firmly believe that they're absolutely essential to the creation of meaningful friendships.

Back in the Montessori classroom, Violet finally extricated herself from Marquis's embrace and called Tal and me over to show off her recent work. I was expecting a tour through her items from the Completed Lessons board, but instead, she led us to a corner of the room, and pointed toward a low, metal shelf. "This is the art display," she said.

Marquis had trailed us quietly, and as he emerged, he innocuously but infectiously offered his forearm for Violet to clutch, the way Harpo Marx was always getting folks to grab hold of his leg. Violet motioned for us all to crouch down and pointed proudly at a row of Popsicle-stick structures. "They're Fairy Houses," she said. "I made them all."

The statement of provenance was unnecessary. The houses—a set of ten or so buildings, each with perfectly pitched roofs and even windows and doors—seemed to reflect Violet's temperament. There was something a bit haunting about seeing them in aggregate, like some Modernist architect's perfectly angular (but unpopulated) design for a city of the future. Yet as I stared more closely at their construction, I spotted some genre-busting details—a crooked lintel here, some bright pink trim there, a foundation line that zigzagged like the tips of a mountain range. It was as if an intriguing cast of looseness was straining to emerge but hadn't yet found its full voice, like in the early figurative work of Phillip Guston or Jackson Pollock.

Violet began explaining which fairies lived in each of her houses, and her descriptions, like the buildings, were nothing if not complete. "This is where the dentist fairy lives; he has his chair and drill right in the house. This is where the garbage collector fairy lives; he has a hose so he can clean his truck." As she spoke, Marquis would chime in every so often, repeating a word or phrase that Violet had spoken—*drill, collector*—as if saying them alond for the first time. Violet would look over at him and smile when he did this, or sometimes add something to his statement. "An archaeologist is also a kind of a collector, right, Marquis?" But after about the fifth house, the boy became restless. Sensing this, Violet stopped her tour and turned to us. "Do you want to see Marquis's fairy houses now?" she asked.

We nodded with forced enthusiasm, but as we moved to the far end of the shelving unit—past structures that looked like yurts, bananas, and upturned ice-cream cones—I became intrigued by the possibilities. When we finally stopped, we were standing in front of a shelf that held two extraordinarily disparate buildings. The first looked like an osprey's nest, or maybe an overturned crate of dynamite, that had been slung upside down in a silver macramé plant holder. The other one resembled a cross-section of the Concorde that had been embedded in a trapezpoidal stack of green marshmallows. I was dumbstruck at the jumbled intricacy of the construction—they were made of twigs, string, buttons, wax, foil, papier-mâché, and a sort of gooey foam—as well as by their bizarre consonance. They seemed completely different, but both drew from a similar inspiration: one core element in each being contained or supported by another.

Marquis hadn't seemed like a particularly verbal kid, but when I asked him to tell me about his projects he had quite a bit to say, and when he stumbled, Violet stepped in with cues and prompts.

They talked about the various materials he'd used, about the order in which he'd made the different parts, about the ways he'd engineered things so they'd hold together.

I nodded Marquis along. "And who lives in these Fairy Houses?" I asked.

He thought for only a moment. Then he pointed a finger at himself and one at Violet. "Us," he said, happily. "Violey and me."

I wanted to ask which house he'd intended for whom and why, but just then the teacher called the kids over for circle, which seemed to signal the end of drop-off and the start of the day. Violet joined the crowd on the rug right away, but Marquis lingered at the shelves as if transfixed by his own structures. Eventually, our niece noticed that he was missing and turned to call to him. "Marquis," she bellowed in her booming baritone. "Come on. It's circle time." The boy seemed to hear her as if through the end of giant funnel, and with his eyes still on his buildings, he stumbled blindly toward the sound, the way a dog responds to the noise of a distant but approaching train.

I smiled, charmed by the reality of their connection as well as by what they could potentially offer each other. It wasn't only that their different strengths provided them each with a constructive balance; they actually seemed committed to taking care of one another, and this kind of mutual engagement—with its resultant challenges, its incorporation of divergent strengths, and its voyage into the unknown—seemed at once fascinating and necessary for them both. I sensed somehow that it would make them better people.

"There is no doubt they should have a playdate," I said to Lizzie as we walked toward her office. "Even if it's just so we can videotape him building something."

Lizzie sighed. "Don't start again, okay? Violet's just not that interested. She certainly hasn't ever asked for a *playdate*."

"Well, I'm sure she never asked for a bedtime either, but that doesn't mean you shouldn't give her one." I raised my eyebrows. "Anyway, she's almost four years old. Don't you think it's important for her to learn to engage socially?"

"I suppose," Lizzie sighed. "But what makes you sure we should start with him?"

"Umm . . . because they obviously like one another. Because she's been talking about him at home. Because it seems like they each have something to offer the other."

She rolled her eyes. "Please. He's a disaster waiting to happen. He doesn't listen. He's not careful. He doesn't watch what he's doing. Violet has that open staircase in her room and that window to the roof. I'd be an anxious wreck if he came over."

"So send her to his house."

"You saw his mother. She's too . . . outlandish. Violet would come home with purple highlights or something. No. Forget it. They don't fit."

That's the whole point, I wanted to say. Sure Marquis lived in his own head, and his mother was a

CHECK, PLEASE

YOUR HANDY GUG CHECKLIST FOR:

Knowing When to Have a Playdate

Some kids are innately more social than others. Until they gain a fuller sense of self—usually in their late twos or early threes—most aren't interested in, or capable of, interacting with a peer. They tend to play by themselves or participate in *parallel play*, where they engage in an activity independently but alongside another child. It's your job to watch for the signs that they're ready to start dating. Look for:

❍ *Interest:* Expressing awareness of other kids: how they do things, what they like, how they act

❍ *Selection:* The consistent—and often unremitting—mention of a particular child

❍ *Engagement:* The regular seeking of attention (positive or negative) from specific kids

❍ *Distancing:* The stated or actualized desire to separate from you

fashionista, but he and Violet clearly shared a bond. It was nonlinear and irrational, and it transcended notions of direct or indirect *fit*. But friendship, like so many things for young kids, is like alchemy—the creation of a valuable new substance out of unlikely materials. It's your job as the adult to encourage them to mix, stir, and note the results. Young children are just getting used to the idea that there's a human world that exists beyond themselves, full of other individuals that function in and interpret it in very different ways. Friendship transforms these discoveries, via lived experience, into vital and tangible concepts like perspective, compassion, collusion, and collaboration. Kids need friendships to understand the world.

There's no doubt that kids can pick up bad habits from each other (or other parents) or be exposed to things with which you may not agree. But I think that a good parent (and by that I mean one who follows all the rules laid out in this book) will have imbued their child with a sense of limits and expectations that will allow them to challenge and/or integrate any "negative" influences. And even if there are some minor repercussions, the wondrous benefits of friendship should offset these concerns. Think about it, at age three what's the worst that can happen? They learn the word *fart*? They eat refined sugar? They get exposed to the grating world of Elmo? None of this signals the coming of the apocalypse. It's not as though they're going to rob a bank or start cooking up a batch of crystal meth.

Lizzie didn't say anything for a couple of blocks, until she noticed me staring at a huge flowering magnolia in front of a gorgeous brick row house. "That's where Mary-Alice, this girl in Violet's class, lives," she said. "Her dad runs an environmental-law firm downtown. They just won a big judgment against this awful new power plant."

I nodded. "Maybe Violet could have a playdate over there?"

"I don't think so. I've seen that girl and her cronies in the park. They all wear pink shoes and frilly dresses, and play nothing but Teenager, Mall, and Wedding."

I raised an eyebrow. I wanted to say something like, "If you don't stop worrying about what *kind* of kids Violet can be friends with, she's not going to have the chance to figure out how to make friends *at all*," but I didn't. Lizzie, I knew, had had her own rough social road, trying to negotiate between the sassy but dead-end redneck kids she'd grown up with in the country, and the prissy kids from town with whom she was expected to feel kinship. Her parents hadn't been of much help or guidance, and she was probably looking to spare her daughter some of this. But I wasn't sure she was going about it in the right way. Still, I kept my mouth shut, and we walked Lizzie to her office, making plans to reconvene for lunch. Her building was right across from the art museum, where a banner hung for a show on the Arts and Crafts movement. I nudged Tal and pointed. "Want to have a playdate with me in there?"

He nodded, and squinted over at the banner, which featured a complicated Frank Lloyd Wright structure. "Which of Marquis' houses do you think he made for Violet?"

"The nest," I said. Then I reconsidered. "The crashed plane." I shrugged. "Actually, I don't know. Which do you think suits her best?"

Tal smiled. "Honestly, I could see her living in either one of them."

I grabbed his forearm. "Me too." I told him my thoughts about Violet's need for a playdate and my theories about Lizzie and Ace's difficulties in letting go. Tal promised to wage a stealth campaign to convince them.

"But if they do get together," Tal said, as we entered the

museum, "you better hope he doesn't teach her any bad habits."
He watched as a school group clustered, tittering, around a
medieval set of equine armor; one outlier girl was staring enrap-
tured at a nearby garbage can. "On second thought," he said, "I
hope he does."

GUG'S TIPS FOR HANDLING:

Friendship

Peer-based interpersonal interaction is paramount for young children's proper development. So regardless of whether you think all the kids your child meets are greedy, ignorant bitches, it's worthwhile for you to encourage connections. I know the process can be humiliating and can hearken back to your own devastating childhood social experiences. But buck up. The rewards outweigh the risks.

- *What's Your Sign:* Some kids are shy, others are outgoing, but all kids benefit from social interaction. Watch for signals that your child is interested in engaging with other kids, but don't feel the need to force them before they're ready. Learning to be open to others takes time.

- *Name It:* Like those chimps at the zoo picking lice off of each other, humans are social animals at heart. Still, kids don't automatically know what a "friend" is. You can help them figure this out, even very early on, by naming the actions and behaviors that signify friendship. "He's sharing his sandwich with her because they're friends." Point them out in everyday exchanges, or in books or movies.

- *Demonstrate:* Kids learn best by experience or example. This means that one of the ways you can help your child comprehend the concept of friendship is by having them spend time with you and your friends. It's just the excuse you've always been looking for! "Honey, I'd love to stay in and do the laundry with you, but I have to go over to Brett's house with the baby and model pro-social behaviors."

- *Home In:* I know that it's embarrassing and nerve-wracking to play host to strangers, or to consider siccing your ill-behaved offspring on someone else, but there's no better way for your kid to bridge the home/peer barrier than for them to share their *home* with a *peer* (or vice versa). One of the key things kids learn from playdates is how to respond to and integrate new behavioral standards, so feel confident that disciplining that rowdy friend is actually helping to "educate" them.

- *Not My Friend:* You are an adult with (hopefully) your own social life (see chapter 1), so just because your child has chosen a friend doesn't mean you have to like that kid's parents—especially if they're stupid or boring. If the grown-ups irk you, offer to host a playdate without them or to take the kids out for some special event. This avoids awkward interactions and earns you reciprocity. Plus, if you don't like them, chances are they probably don't like you either; the separation will be a relief to everyone involved.

- *Good, Better, Best, Bested:* Encourage your child to have a wide range of friends and allow for the idea that they may want to spend more time with some than with others. But also know that naming someone a "best" friend at this age often creates a ticking bomb—a way of setting up a conflict or competition or fall from grace. Better your kid should have a bunch of *good* friends than one contentious *best* friend.

SAY "UNCLE!"

10.
Put Turkey Baby Back
New Siblings

WE DIDN'T MEET Athena, Kate and Dylan's second child, until she was already a few months old. Granted, I'd been traveling nonstop for work that spring, and melding our schedules was difficult, but the same had been true when their son Max was born, and I seemed to recall that we'd managed to meet him less than a week after he'd joined the ranks of the air breathers. As it happened, this turned out to be standard operating procedure. Parents treat the arrival of a first child the way a city prepares to host the Olympics: announcements are made, banners are hung, and hotel rooms are booked—all egregiously in advance of the actual event. But subsequent births have a markedly lower degree of pomp, something more akin to the excitement generated by a visit from one's accountant. There are no showers. There are no birth videos (thank god). There are no e-mailed links to online Web cams that allow you to "watch in real time as our beloved sleeps."

I happen to think this is a healthier attitude. Few people ultimately benefit from being treated like a messiah. (Look how the world responded to that Jesus character.) Plus, the eggshell dance of having a first child tends to break parents in and give them a little perspective, so they're less likely to be as stuck in the **PARENTING BUBBLE** with the second. This often renders child number two better adjusted in comparison. (Full disclosure: I'm a second child. *We try harder!*)

We finally met up with Kate and Dylan and the baby on a spring afternoon in the park by their place uptown. The actual catalyst for our picnic was celebrating Tal's and Kate's birthdays, both of which fell on the same day, but it was a good excuse to bring Athena along. Our friends were late, and when they finally arrived, the girl was asleep, Though I didn't say so, this is how I prefer to meet babies. It allows you to *ooh* and *aah* and deliver the obligatory lies about how much she favors her parents' best features, without being interrupted from socializing. In fact, we'd nearly finished lunch and the first bottle of wine before we got around to talking about Athena at all. They told us about her excellent sleep schedule (soon to change; see chapter 4), her infrequent feedings, and how good-natured she was. This was boring. I wanted conflict. I thrive on conflict. So I probed. "How's Max handling the arrival of his new little sister?"

Sensing my bloodlust, Kate didn't answer. We loved their son Max—he was goofy and adorable—but we still treated him like something that had come between all of us, an invader of the space we'd once occupied in their lives, and thus responded to his actions with the mixture of prurience and resentment usually reserved for the new boyfriend of one's ex-boyfriend. This didn't make my curiosity any less genuine, but since Kate's lips remained pursed I added encouragement. "Really. We want to know."

She shrugged. "It's going okay, I guess."

Dylan screwed up his face. "Please. He wants to kill her. He tries nearly every time he sees her. He usually starts off with something resembling affection, but then it almost immediately takes a dastardly turn. Stroking her arm becomes twisting it. Playing with her toys morphs to smashing her with them. Even his hugs are attempts at suffocation."

"We're afraid," Kate said, "that we've ruined his life."

I nodded and tried to act concerned, but three things prevented this from coming off as totally honest. First, I knew that sibling rivalry was normal and thus expected that they'd be dealing with it. Second, I was sort of pleased that Max's primacy was being challenged (oh, how the mighty have fallen) as it mimicked and supplanted my own sense of being displaced from our best friends' lives—by him. And third, I remembered that when

Adding Siblings

While there's nothing wrong having only one kid, sibling rivalry shouldn't be your primary concern in determining whether or not to have another. There are plenty of other more important factors to consider in bringing new life into this world, like global environmental degradation or the mercilessly inexorable nature of Robin Williams's acting career. The question therefore shouldn't be whether *your child* can handle the addition of a new sibling but whether *you* can—emotionally, financially, physically, etc. If you lay down a proper foundation and follow through in a consistent way, your kid can definitely learn to deal and share. (You never thought that providing them with more than one parent or caregiver was a valid prohibition on giving birth, did you?) Plus, your children are going to resent you for the rest of their lives anyway, regardless of how many or few of them you have. Providing a sibling will at least give them someone to corroborate the reasons for their resentment, so they don't feel as crazy when they grow up.

Max had been born they'd shared a similar fear about how his arrival had "ruined the life" of their psychotic cats, Brains and Brawn. "You *probably* haven't ruined his life," I said.

I went on to tell my friends that the situation was too well developed to reconsider—they'd already had the baby after all—and so, ruined or not, this was to be Max's life from now on. "So the question isn't whether or not you've made a mistake. The question is how you're handling, and helping him to handle, the change."

Kate looked at Dylan, as if this was a leap. "Well . . . we tell him we still love him."

"Reassurance," I said, nodding her along. "That's good."

"We remind him that Athena's not going to *go away* just because he says he wants her to. That she's going to stay in our family, along with him and us, regardless."

"Demonstrating permanence and modeling adaptive strategies. Also good."

"Sometimes we let him pick out her clothes when he's choosing what he wants to wear that day. He likes to dress them in matching outfits. Pink outfits."

Tal brightened. "Oh my god. He is *such* a little fag."

Kate shrugged. "We know."

I concurred, delighted. "But the clothing thing is actually good," I said. "You're getting him invested in her well-being. You're giving him tasks that set them apart *and* connect them. And you're involving him in caring for her in ways he can achieve. Now you've just got to get him doing her hair and makeup, and pretty soon he'll be supporting you as a stylist." I smiled. "Really, it sounds like you're doing fine."

Dylan tapped Kate's knee. "Tell him about the turkey."

"Oh, right. I was making a turkey at Easter, and the kids were both with me in the kitchen. Being *gay,* Max is obviously fascinated with cooking, so he was watching as I cleaned the bird and reached in to get that vile bag of organs they leave inside. I'd never made a turkey before—I was on the phone with my grandma the entire morning getting instructions—so when he asked me what I was doing, I panicked and went for a laugh, and as I pulled out the gut sack, I said I was taking out the turkey's baby. I even made grunting noises like the turkey was giving birth. This was a big hit and he asked me to 'put turkey baby back' and perform this birth sequence again, but after I'd stuffed and delivered it twice more, the bag started to leak, and I called an end to the game. He was disappointed and got real quiet for a minute, but then he looked over at his sister, and this sinister grin came across his face. 'Put Thena back?' he asked, brightly."

I laughed hysterically, but once I calmed myself down, I reminded them that the birth was a big deal for Max and that they had to expect some fallout. "Still, it sounds like you're on the right track," I said. "The big thing is to keep a sense of balance. You have to validate his notion that things have changed, while letting him know that his new sister's presence is inalienable. Make it clear that you love him as much as you always did, but make sure he recognizes that he's going to have to learn to share you."

Our friends nodded blankly, like this was too general an order, and I tried to come up with more specific advice. The truth was, as effective as ex post facto actions could be, sibling rivalry (like most things with young kids) is best dealt with preemptively, and it was becoming clear that Kate and Dylan hadn't laid much groundwork ahead of time.

I thought about the proactive ways we handled the issue at my school. Inevitably, during the course of the year, a few kids would be dealing with the imminent arrival of a new sibling, and since all of our curricular explorations grew from the kids' interests and experiences, the approaching birth became cause for an in-depth study of the subject.

We went about our investigations in many different ways, but we usually started out by making two lists: one of what we already knew about the topic and one containing the questions we wanted to have answered. In the baby curriculum, this first step usually resulted in the kids coming up with an inventory of baby behaviors: they poop in diapers, they cry instead of using words, they sleep in cribs, they breast-feed, etc. This catalog of attributes not only provided context for our understanding of what a baby *is*, it also helped the kids learn to sort and categorize—to define what a baby *isn't*. This type of definition by contrast is an important cognitive skill, and we taught it intentionally in all our curricula. But in this particular version, it had a few added benefits. It helped all the kids in my class differentiate themselves from the category of "baby," an important milestone for a young child's construction of self. And it was also a good way of supporting the soon-to-be older siblings in their need to feel distinct and special within the context of their soon-to-be-growing family.

The next step in our process involved outlining what we wanted to find out. The kids' areas of interest here usually fell along predictable lines as well: Where do babies come from? How are they born? How do they chew without teeth? But they often included a couple of telling ringers: Do they stay babies forever? Once they're born, can they get unborn? Can they ever change from a boy into a girl or a unicorn? We encouraged the kids to come up with a list of diverse resources that we could use to answer these questions: books, field trips, expert interviews. For example, if there was a kid in the class who already had a younger sibling, we made them one of our experts and had them answer their peers' queries based on their experience.

We also tried to make the arrival of a classmate's new sibling fun and exciting—in addition to teaching some basic evolutionary biology—with a proprietary "prediction" game we developed. Using photos of our classmate and their parents as our starting point, we had the kids try to guess what color the new baby's skin, hair, and eyes would be, and we'd chart these speculations on a big piece of paper. Once the baby was born, we'd compare these guesses with the actual product, either by inviting the newborn in for a first-hand study, or taking a field trip to the kid's house to see it in its native habitat. Regardless of whether or not anyone's predictions were right, we'd hold a Big Brother/Sister party for the older sibling to imprint the event with a celebratory stamp.

In addition, the school had the advantage of being just a short bus ride away from New York University Hospital, and a field trip to its neonatal ward was always part of the curriculum. One year, we went with a girl in my class named Daphne, a loquacious four-year-old, who seemed to squint curiously at just about everything. Daphne's younger sister was going to be born at NYU in just a few weeks, making the trip even more resonant.

Since I wanted to give Daphne some extra attention during this excursion, I knelt down beside her as she peered through the ward's big picture window and let her know that I was there to answer any questions she might have. With all of the blue or pink swaddled infants lined up in matching cribs, and the nurses in biohazard suits moving about among them adjusting, feeding, wrapping, and rewrapping, the place felt like something out of a Michael Crichton novel—a factory in which the newborns were being groomed as prey. But since the kids in my class seemed to view it more like the fresh donuts window at Krispy Kreme—New Batch Ready Now!—I did my best to hide my horror. Late in the visit, one of the nurses shuffled in, walked over to a baby, and unceremoniously took it away. Daphne looked at me with mischievous intent. "Where are they taking it . . . ?" she asked, thoughts of a garbage can or a distant planet clearly dancing in her head.

I gave Kate and Dylan a shortened version of all this. Knowing that Max was struggling a bit with mastering things like sleeping through the night and recovering when things didn't go his way, I put a particular emphasis on the ideas of celebrating the distinctions between him and his little sister. Kids often benefit from a bit of a push, and I had seen their efforts to distinguish themselves from a new sibling act as this kind of catalyst, providing a child with the incentive to release and move forward. I told Kate and Dylan that I'd once had an Algerian girl named Fatima in my class. Though she understood English perfectly, her parents spoke to her solely in French at home, and so she'd always had a certain verbal shyness at school. She also had a low frustration threshold and frequently retreated into tears, earning her a reputation as a crybaby. Once her little brother Alex was born, however, she began to change. Within a few weeks of his arrival, she became more outgoing and even began using words to resolve her conflicts. Her parents noticed this transformation as well, and when we spoke about it I suggested that she had likely made these leaps, in part, as a way of distinguishing herself from her newborn brother.

Kate looked at me dubiously. "If anything, Max seems to be heading in the other direction. He wants to sleep in the baby's crib. He wants his baby toys back. He wants me to dress him in his old onesies."

"That's interesting," I said. "Let me ask you a question. Is the crib Athena sleeps in the one he used when he was little?"

"Yeah."

"And the toys she's playing with? And the clothes she's wearing?"

"Of course. Christ, we're not made of money. We're not going to buy all new baby stuff. That shit's expensive."

"I don't think you should buy all new things," I said. "In fact, as you know, I'm opposed to most of the things you already have. [See chapter 3.] But I'm wondering if you talked to Max at all before handing over all of his old possessions?"

"Possessions? Please. They were in the storage space in the basement. He hasn't mentioned them in months. And he wasn't exactly *using* them."

"True enough," I said. Indeed, Max may have "forgotten" about these things, but on seeing them it seemed logical that he'd still consider them his. "And he'd be irritated and jealous," I told Kate, "that they'd been given away, without his involvement, and to his new rival. Let's put it this way: my closet is full of things that I no longer wear, things that are too small or youthful for me to realistically put on ever again, but I would be pissed to hell if Tal suddenly donated them to some younger, cuter friend of his. Though it's irrational, I might even want them back. You'd probably do the same."

"Okay," Kate said. "Fine. You got me. I'm a bad mother."

"I didn't say that."

"Yeah, but it sounds like it's too late for me do any of what you *did* say."

"It's *never* too late to start."

Hand-Me-Downs

So many things in your child's life are constantly changing that stable objects tend to provide them with a sense of security about their world. Knowing to whom objects belong, and which objects go with which person, also helps kids develop means of categorizing and making sense of issues of identity: doctors have stethoscopes so they can listen to your heartbeat; babies drink from bottles because they don't have teeth; I have a toy horse because I like horses. Kids can certainly be flexible and resilient about objects changing hands, but it really helps if you involve them directly in this process, especially with things that they believe belong to them. The fact that they may have forgotten about such objects only makes their reappearance (particularly in someone else's hands) all the more disorienting. *You* think you're being efficient and practical, *they* feel a rupture in their understanding of the world. Instead of unilaterally picking out things to give to the new baby, take your older child with you to where you keep their old stuff (it helps if you've involved them in putting it away here in the first place), explain the process, and have them help you locate things that they've outgrown but that might be suitable for a newborn. Regression is normal, so don't be surprised if they want to revive things for their own use. You can even let them pick out one or two. But stay focused and remember: you're in charge.

"If I'm not mistaken," Tal added, "these kids are going to be around for a while."

Dylan pulled a box of cookies from under the stroller, signaling that our get-together was winding down, and we started making a plan to meet out on some distant Saturday night. This discussion seemed to remind Dylan of something important and he nudged Kate, and mumbled, "Ask him about Romalia."

Kate rolled her eyes. Romalia was Max's former babysitter, a Polish lady who somewhat resembled Joan Crawford—if Joan Crawford had been born a man. She'd always struck me as a strange choice for a child's first caregiver. She walked with a cane, spoke in a monotone, and rarely smiled, but though Max didn't like her, she was always available on Saturday nights and she was nothing if not consistent—she was practically a robot. As with most of these master–servant relationships, my friends were uncomfortable bossing her around, so despite the fact that she was always making racist comments, that they caught her feeding meat to their vegetarian son, and that she spent most Saturday nights ignoring Max and IM'ing her many Czech paramours, they used her exclusively for almost a year. "What about her?" I asked Kate. "Did you finally get a letter from the INS confirming that she actually *did* run the children's wing at Auschwitz?"

"She wasn't so bad."

"Compared to Pol Pot."

Kate sneered. Apparently, since Athena was born, whenever she or Dylan announced that they were planning to go out, Max would howl and scream that he wanted Romalia. They'd since found some more appropriate sitters, including an African American theater major named Candi who lived on buppie movies and junk food (two thumbs up from me and Tal) and Terri, a petrifyingly sincere nursing student who was allergic to anything with a scent

(K&D's top choice—no doubt in part because it gave them an excuse to buy exclusive, olfactorially inoffensive household products that they had to special-order from Sweden). Still, when departure time arrived, the boy would beg for Romalia. Inevitably, things would escalate into a full-scale battle, in which Max would cling to their legs and make faces at the scheduled sitter and which they would try to win—with dogged, but futile, rationality—by making up lies about Romalia's lack of availability and reminding him of her endemic faults.

"So, what do we do?" Dylan asked.

I tried to give them my usual pointers about sitters (see chapter 1), but they'd heard it all before. Plus, they were too emotional, and too stuck in their **PARENTING BUBBLE** to be open to reason. Their heartstrings were being strummed. "It feels like, first we abandon him symbolically by giving him a sister he doesn't want," Kate said. "Then we abandon him physically by going out every weekend. Then we cap it all off by sticking him with some new grown-up he doesn't even like. I'm actually thinking about calling Romalia."

I nodded and gave the situation some thought, and it wasn't long before I came up with a hypothesis. As with his reaction to their giving Athena his old toys and crib, it seemed that part of what Max might be responding to with his Romalia quest was some vague notion of the loss of his infancy, which he'd begun to feel was slipping away—rapidly, and forever.

Young kids don't understand change the way we do. They've not yet developed the capacity for abstract or analytical thought, so they lack the ability to create an external perspective on their situation, to summarize and codify it into a statement or concept: "I'm sad because . . ." Plus, regardless of whether or not they possess this skill, they're frequently powerless to change, or even to understand *how* to change, their circumstance. Given all this swirling confusion, it's not surprising that their responses to things don't follow linear patterns. Whereas we adults might react immediately and directly to the problems posed by a new situation—Trouble with an officious new co-worker? Put tacks on her chair!—a child will often move through that change without fully comprehending its impact, leaving the effects to reveal themselves in other, often seemingly unrelated, realms.

Max had begun to observe the ways that he was different and distinct from his new sibling—*not* sleeping in a crib, *not* nursing, *not* crying all the time, etc.—and so, though he couldn't name it, he was facing the fact that he was growing up. And while growing up is an exciting process for kids, it's also scary. Since their understanding of the world is grounded in the concrete and the present tense, kids are often uncertain how the world will respond to changes in their capabilities. For example, kids can struggle with learning to read in part because they worry that once they know how, no one will read aloud to them anymore; or they can have a hard time giving up their baby habits out of fear that if they do, they'll no longer be taken care of the way they're used to. Max's quest for the familiar aspects of his infancy—his crib, his old sitter—reflected his attempt to ask the world and his parents (the people ostensibly in charge of the world) who he was now and what that means: to explore the boundaries of his changing sense of self.

Athena suddenly started to stir, and our friends got up abruptly, needing to rush her home for a scheduled feeding. This ended our get-together, but before they left I gave them one last piece of advice. Though it felt like a betrayal of my instinctual mistrust, I suggested that the next time they went out, they should consider hiring Romalia. I wasn't at all sure what the end-up of this reunion would be, but—as with the time when I tried to set up my newly divorced mother up with my best friend's newly divorced father, or when I first tried mixing snorkeling with drinking—I had the sense that it might catalyze something interesting.

I was swamped with work over the next couple of weeks, but one afternoon I received an e-mail from my older brother containing the patronizing subject heading "Little Bro," and it reminded me to check in on the situation with Max and Athena, and Romalia. I zipped a quick e-mail over to Kate and Dylan. I'm compulsive about communication and usually answer e-mails within hours. In contrast, the two of them were famous for tardy to nonexistent responses, so it was surprising when Kate wrote back right away.

"We had Romalia come over two days after we saw you," she wrote. "Max apparently fought with her from the moment she arrived until the moment he collapsed on the floor in exhaustion. But we've gone out twice since then, and he hasn't made a peep about staying with Terri or Candi.

thanks for SHARING

One Tiny GUG Minute On: Nonlinear Development

Kids don't develop linearly. This means that while they often gain skills that build on each other in a serial manner (crawling leads to walking; babbling leads to talking), they don't necessarily give up every aspect of the old skill set as soon as they've mastered the new one. Since they have difficulty projecting into the future, young children need to constantly explore and retrench in order to find the borders of what feels safe. It is therefore not at all uncommon for a child to regress when undergoing change (to have a spate of "accidents" after learning to use the bathroom) or to counter their achievement in one area with a backsliding in another (to have a spate of "accidents" while successfully adapting to starting school). On top of this is the simple issue of their capabilities: *they're little; they can only keep so much under control at once.* A child's development is like that arcade game Whac-A-Mole: they nail something down in one realm, and another issue either pops up elsewhere or in the exact same place. It is your job to reassure them, to help them understand change, and to let them know what and where the boundaries are. To be faux Zen about it: you have to teach them not to fear the mole.

Plus, he's stopped bashing Athena's head against the kitchen floor (for now). He's actually been kind of sweet to her recently."

I wrote back right away, telling her not to get too used to this cease-fire. "Max has worked through something (for now), but some other problem is bound to rear up."

"Thanks!" Kate wrote back. I could feel the comforting embrace of her sarcasm.

GUG'S TIPS FOR HANDLING:
A New Sibling

Sibling rivalry *will* happen. But your child is less likely to respond negatively to the new baby's birth—and thus less likely to develop negative patterns with their new sibling—if you follow these steps.

- *Start Early:* Once you start telling your friends that you're pregnant, tell your kid. Though they're often unable to articulate it, kids are very attuned to changes in the way people close to them behave, and if they're not told why, it can unmoor them. (Also, you don't want them to think Mommy's just let herself go.) Be open: talk about the pregnancy, discuss its effects, find age-appropriate books on the subject. Kids are much more likely to be scared of what they *don't* know than what they *do.*

- *Make It a Process:* Kids are more able to enjoy, understand, and integrate information if it's presented as a step-by-step process. If you point out a pretty flower in someone's garden, they may shrug and walk by—or pluck off its head. If they're involved in watching that flower grow from a seed, they become drawn into its development and the end product becomes their own. (Are you catching on to this subtle metaphor?) Post a calendar with the due date and have them count down the days; show them the sonogram pictures; have them measure and chart Mom's growing belly. Think increments.

- *Embroil Them:* Your child is accustomed to much of the activity in your home being focused around *them.* When this shifts, they can feel abandoned or ignored, which can cause anxiety, anger, and jealousy. If they're enlisted to help, they feel useful and know they're still a central part of the action. I know they're slow, messy, and unfocused, but I'm sure you can find things for them to do.

- *Differentiate:* Kids can feel displaced by the excitement surrounding a new baby—as if you've traded them in for a newer, cuter model. A new sibling can also bring up issues in their own identity development. ("I'm still in diapers. Does this mean *I'm* still a baby?") Counter this by making sure to give them plenty of attention and also by playing up the ways they're distinct from the new baby: more capable, bigger, more grown-up. Give them new responsibilities that reflect or enhance this sense. Even small things, like letting a child turn off their own light, can make them feel more mature.

- *Expect Issues:* Your older child will be sharing you in ways they're not used to. This is a *big* change and will take time to integrate. Have the expectation that they will behave properly, but don't be too surprised or horrified if they say or do something against the new baby. To find their balance and discover their place in the new family dynamic, they may need to test the boundaries. Be prepared to let them know where these are—probably much more than once.

- *Respond Appropriately:* If you fly off the handle when flare-ups happen, you older child may see this as a way to get a big dose of the attention they feel they've lost. This will set a negative pattern. Instead, be clear and firm with your limits, be empathetic to their feelings, and find a way to positively redirect their energies: "I understand that you don't like sharing me with your sister, but biting her while I'm nursing isn't an okay way to get my attention. I'm always happy to give you a hug. You just need to ask. After that, I could really use your help burping her."

SAY "UNCLE!"

11.
Drop and Ditch
Starting School

CLARISSE ASKED FOR my commitment point-blank. I was in Baltimore for work and had arranged to stay an extra night so I could visit with her and her husband, Miguel, and as we were sitting in the living room of their gentrifier's paradise—a row house in an up-and-coming section of the city—she sighed and made the request. "I'm going to look at a school for Katia tomorrow. I want you to come with me and tell me what you think."

Other friends had made similar overtures before, though they were usually much more subtle. "What are some things I should be watching for in a teacher?" "What's your view on Montessori?" "Do you think it's a bad sign if the school has a stockade?" But Clarisse and I had always been quite direct. Our best friends had dated each other in college, leaving us to form a couple of our own, and we'd quickly developed a rapport based on brutal honesty. She was one of the few people I could tell, "You look awful in those pants," and she never failed to correct me when my behavior veered out of bounds.

I didn't at all mind visiting schools. When I was

running a preschool, I used to offer this service to the parents whose kids were aging out of my center. I would go on tours at the local schools and provide feedback about their potential fit. But I always went on these expeditions alone so I could gather my own subjective impressions. I was worried what it might be like to have a parent, and their **BUBBLE**, along for the ride.

Still, I couldn't very well say no. One of the side effects of Clarisse's honesty was that it disarmed my ability to lie. Plus, I'd already given the next morning over to her, planning to hang out until my 1 p.m. train. Finally, there was the whole issue of payback: Clarisse's husband was a urologist at a public clinic and had given me a free, and very *private,* phone consultation the previous fall when I was dealing with an embarrassing issue that we won't discuss here. "Sure," I said, lightly. "That'd be fun."

I hadn't seen their nearly two-year-old daughter, Katia, in a while, so I spent some time the next morning reacquainting myself with her. After she'd finished eating, we read a book together, and she showed me some of her favorite toys: a magic wand, a toy pony, a tiny glow-in-the-dark skeleton. She seemed quiet but interested, and interesting. Then we all bundled up against the spring chill and took her to the home day care she currently attended. It was a small, diverse group, made up of five kids her age, and was run by an energetic, warm, and no-nonsense older woman. I liked it right away and could see it was a good match for Katia. I told Clarisse this, which seemed to put her at ease; she'd often expressed concern about placing her daughter in day care so young.

After dropping Katia off, Clarisse drove us over to the school we'd be visiting: an early childhood center that was affiliated with the local public pre-K program. It was housed on the first floor of the neighborhood grade school, and the building had a classic urban public school feel: it was big and rectilinear, with high ceilings and windows, and long hallways punctuated by colonnades of doors. The plaster walls were painted shades of blue, yellow, and green that could only be described as institutional.

Having spent time in literally hundreds of schools—as a teacher, administrator, and educational researcher—my gut sense of what a school is like develops quite rapidly: I can quickly tell if the kids are engaged, if the teachers seem driven and supported, if the administration is accessible and involved. It's a total impression, based on a multitude of factors, including a deep understanding of the possibilities of school settings and how these function for the people who inhabit them. Needless to say, this impression is often very different from what a parent sees. Imagine the disparities in the way a mechanic and consumer might view a used car. The consumer may see what's on the surface: a clean interior, low mileage, and well-maintained paint. But a mechanic will see beneath this as well: if a car is listing, if the exhaust smells of burning antifreeze, or if the low odometer reading doesn't match the highly worn tires.

thanks for SHARING

One Tiny GUG Minute On: Child Care for Kids Under Age Two

Given my professional experience, it should come as no surprise that I believe quality child-care settings can be appropriate and beneficial, even for very young kids. But I do have a few caveats on this practice.

1. Children under age two require more individuated care, so I recommend a single or shared (and consistent) caregiver or a small-group setting (fewer than six children) for kids this age.

2. You'll notice that I said *quality* childcare setting. The site should conform to high standards: with a well-trained and experienced staff, developmentally appropriate practices, and a safe and child-friendly space. (For a definition of *quality*, check out the Early Childhood Program Standards at the Web site of the National Association for the Education of Young Children, www.naeyc.org.)

One Tiny *GUG* Minute On: School Buildings

Parents often respond to school buildings very differently from the way that children or teachers do. Here's how to debunk a few common misconceptions:

- *So Big:* Your child may initially be wary of any large, unfamiliar space. But kids are adept at creating a manageable sense of scale by ignoring things that aren't proximal or relevant. Their classroom becomes a source of intimacy and their sense of the building shrinks around this.

- *It's Institutional:* These spaces often feel cold to us because of past associations. But navigating these buildings often gives kids a sense of accomplishment.

- *Sheer Chaos:* Young children need to be hands-on and physical in order to learn. In a good school, there will be an underlying order to the chaos—and someone who can explain this to you. A noisy preschool shouldn't necessarily scare you; a silent one definitely should.

I got a very positive sense from the school right away. The kids in the hall looked comfortable but not without order; the teachers spoke to them in a clear and warm manner, but one that lacked signs of exhaustion or false sweetness; and from what I could see, the layout of the early-childhood wing—on the ground floor, past a security check, away from the big kids—felt conscientious and deliberate. But given how Clarisse scrunched up her nose, she clearly didn't feel the same way. So when she began to make disparaging comments about the school's scale, style, and setup I felt obliged to counter.

A friendly administrator greeted us to lead the tour—this seemed like another positive sign: she was hands-on, not leaving it up to some lackey from the PTA—and my first impression held as we entered a classroom. It was "work time"—the major chunk of action during the preschool day, when the kids get to engage with the different materials—and there were clusters of kids all around the room: at the water table, at the art area, doing dramatic play, building with blocks. Every center was occupied by a diverse and mixed-gender group, something that struck a chord with me. I've seen way too many racially or ethnically segregated schools and/or classes where the boys dominate the room with violent play, leaving the girls to cower in the dress-up area. A proper mix like this doesn't happen on its own and indicated to me that the school and teachers were actively involved in challenging destructive social norms. As capper, there was a head teacher and two assistants present: for a group of eighteen three-year-olds, a very suitable ratio.

I leaned in to give Clarisse my initial thumbs-up, but I immediately noticed that her nose was still scrunched. "You're scowling," I whispered. "No one likes a scowler." I reminded her that the school was auditioning *her* as well and that a bad attitude would likely be a strike against her. "Put your game face on," I said.

"I thought I *was* wearing my game face."

"Well, then it's for the wrong game." I demonstrated a properly interested nod.

Clarisse sighed and corrected herself, drawing her lips together in a way that made her look attentive. But, knowing her as long as I had, I could tell she was faking. When I followed her eye, she seemed to be focused on a solitary Latino girl who was thumbing through a copy of *Caps for Sale* in a cozy reading nook by the bookshelf. "She looks so lonely," Clarisse said. "Why doesn't the teacher do something?"

"Like what? Take her book away and force her to join that tea party?" I pointed to the opposite side of the room, where a cluster of kids were gathered around a table. "Sustained exposure to books is key to the development of emergent literacy skills."

"Don't edu-talk down to me," Clarisse said, frowning. "She's sad."

Like most of my friends, Clarisse had been a social outsider as a kid—a debater, a tap dancer, a chess-club member—and I could tell she was overidentifying with this girl, imagining her as dejected. But the girl looked engaged and content to me, mouthing the words to the story. "Kids don't have to be social to have a good time," I said. "A quality classroom will provide opportunities for solitary *and* group play."

Clarisse grunted. "Well, then I'm going to observe some *group play*. By myself."

Since she clearly needed some space, I walked to the opposite side of the room. I watched a girl drawing with crayons and then a group of kids working with manipulatives: literally trying to fit a round peg into a square hole. They were doing a nice job sharing the materials, which spoke well to what we call the "culture of the classroom"—the tenor and tone of personal interactions—and I thought to wave Clarisse over to come and see, but when I looked for her she was back by the book nook, talking to our tour guide. Because of her candid approach to conversation, Clarisse often came off as brusque, and I worried that the woman would feel cross-examined, but instead she seemed charmed by my friend's odd directness: laughing and reassuring her. I smiled. As a teacher and director, I'd been drawn to the weird and neurotic parents too. They were much more compelling than the ones who were disinterested or hands-off.

Clarisse appeared to have warmed to the place, and as we left and headed for lunch at a restaurant by the train station, I listed the reasons for my own positive assessment: that it had a sound philosophy, appropriate practices, a nice mix of kids, attentive staff, and a good child–teacher ratio (see Check, Please, page 194).

"On top of that," I said, "it seems like it would be a good fit for Katia, who's sort of teetering on engagement but needing something to pull her out of her shell."

Clarisse nodded appreciatively at my analysis, but the closer we got to the restaurant, the less convinced she seemed. She was pulling back. "What are you stuck on?" I finally asked, after we ordered. "What were you talking about with the director?"

"That Latino girl." Clarisse threw up her hands. "I'm sorry, okay? I just can't help but feel that, based on what I saw, Katia won't get enough attention there."

I'd heard this issue many times—from friends, from prospective parents, even from people who had no experience with kids but wanted to give their two cents on our educational system. Over the course of my tenure in early childhood, I'd developed a pointed response, which was based on exposing our cultural bias against collectivism.

"Compulsory public education," I told Clarisse, "was initially considered a radical socialist plot in this country, and that heritage lingers. It's still the only universal, national support system we have. But because we don't believe in these kinds of group solutions, we have an inherent mistrust of it. And because we don't have any other experience with these kinds of group solutions, we don't know how to respond when we deal with it. It's why we have so much inequity in the system—special schools for the gifted, and *un*special schools for the *un*gifted—as well as things like the explosion of all these homeschoolers."

Clarisse held her hands up in surrender. "Okay, okay. I reconsider." She glanced at her BLT. "Though I must admit, the idea of homeschooling *has* crossed my mind."

I pointed at her. "Don't get me started. Homeschooling is the ultimate version of placing the needs of the individual over those of the group. Schools rely on a wide mix of kids, with all sorts of different abilities and intelligences, to help everyone thrive. If kids opt out, they're not able to gain from, or give to, the knowledge base of the group. And if the most driven kids opt out, the system

CHECK, PLEASE

YOUR HANDY GUG CHECKLIST FOR:

Selecting a School / Day Care

There are all sorts of schools out there, and the criteria for choosing one can feel overwhelming. But the best way to understand how schools work is to see them in action. You don't want to be one of those people who start touring preschools before they're pregnant. But you also don't want to be knocking on doors in August desperately seeking a spot for September. Different locations have different standards, but it wouldn't hurt to start arranging tours the winter or spring before you want your child to start. Visit the schools where your friends send their kids, visit the schools your friends *didn't* choose, visit the same school more than once. But don't feel the need to become a 360-degree expert: after all, you don't have to understand aeronautics and navigation to fly safely from New York to LA. Remember that an elemental part of picking the right school is choosing one in which you have a *blind* trust.

Here are some things to look for and ask about as you make your rounds.

○ *Child—Teacher Ratio:* Infants/toddlers, 1:1 or 2:1; two-year-olds, 3:1 or 4:1; three- to five-year-olds, 5:1 or 6:1

○ *Teacher Training:* Training doesn't tell you everything, but it can help you get a sense of how schools select their staff. The head teacher should have *at least* a bachelor's degree in early childhood education. Assistant teachers should have *at least* an associate's degree or training certificate.

○ *Daily Schedule:* There should be a regular pattern to each day and a thoughtful and explicable reasoning behind its flow. There should also be time *every day* for structured *and* unstructured play; full group, small group, *and* solitary activities; and indoor *and* outdoor experiences.

○ *Curriculum:* Good schools focus on teaching kids how to learn, and on giving them the skills to explore and develop knowledge, as opposed to solely filling them with facts. Identification—of letters, objects, etc.—is important for young kids, but it is one of the lower-order thinking skills. Look for a school that also asks kids to strive for higher-order thinking skills: differentiation, analysis, inference, experimentation, integration, explanation, and reaching conclusions, Ask about *how* the school inspires a child to *think,* instead of *what* the school asks or expects a child to *know.*

CHECK, PLEASE

○ *Warmth:* Kids need to feel cared for by the adults around them, and they need to know that those adults are safe. Different teachers have different styles, so this doesn't always mean physical affection (though I'd be wary of a place that totally ruled that out). But you should be able to sense the respect and connection between the teachers and the kids at all times, even when a child is being disciplined.

○ *Materials:* Kids learn best from directed, open-ended play with simple materials like blocks, clay, art supplies, and manipulatives. These allow them to bring their lived experiences into the classroom, to have ownership over the creation of knowledge, to experiment, and to learn by trial and error. Look for materials that provide opportunities for investigation, imagination, and repeated and deepening appreciation. Beware of materials that have only one use, or a single "right or wrong" way of being used.

○ *The "Real" World:* People often said disparagingly of the preschool I ran that it "isn't like the real world." Well, guess what? I think the real world sucks. It's crumbling and cruel and ruled by ignorant bullies. Why would anyone want to replicate that, particularly in the service of molding the minds of impressionable young children? I believe that intentional environments, like a preschool, should be as ideal and humane as possible. This means having rules to ensure that all its members are respected and providing them with recourse for when they feel harmed or excluded. It is only by challenging the hideous and brutal practices of the so-called real world that we can actually effect real change.

parenting bubble ALERT!

Individuals in School

Parents are often concerned that their child won't get enough attention in a school setting. I respect this fear but firmly believe that it's rooted in our national antagonism toward collective situations. In America, we believe that the individual is king: it's at the core of our most vital national myths, from the cowboy to the self-made man. Schools, however, are concerned with collective good: with working together to balance the needs of the individual with the larger goals of the good of the group, and of society. A quality school will make sure that each child is attended to within this context, but even the best schools by necessity and design will ask parents, kids, and teachers to sacrifice some of their individual desires for the benefit of the whole. Parents often see this solely as a deficit. But education exists not simply to serve individual needs but also to help foster group achievement, as well as to develop practices that are key to the smooth functioning of civil society.

suffers exponentially, and if the system suffers, we all suffer. It's like the United States opting out of the Kyoto Accords on global warming, because we don't think it's *good for us*. Hello. We all live on the same earth. How *good* is it going to be for *us* if it's all underwater?" I raised my eyebrows.

I had to rush out of the restaurant to make my train and left Clarisse sitting there, reeling in the wake of my diatribes. I hoped I'd put the fear of the educator gods into her, and I hoped they'd help her make the right decisions for herself and her family. But I didn't hear from her for a while, so I wasn't sure how she resolved things. It wasn't uncommon for us to go for long stretches without talking, and we were always able to pick up where we left off, so I was delighted to get her e-mail early that fall, saying she was coming up to New York for a conference. "Let's meet/catch up," she wrote. I recommended a Korean place near her hotel, and she confirmed immediately.

When I arrived at the restaurant, she was on the phone. I could tell right away that she was talking to Miguel about Katia, because she was using that panicked, deliberate, and exasperated tone parents often take with their partners. I love these conversations, as they're at once inane and intimate, and reflect the blindness people take on when it comes to their kids: they don't know or care how silly they sound. "Well, did you let her squeeze the ducky a *second* time before you put it in her backpack? She *needs* to squeeze the ducky *two* times!" Clarisse rolled her eyes. I asked the waitress to bring us some beer.

My friend soon hung up, and after toasting our reunion she explained the conversation. Katia had started school three weeks prior—at the program we'd visited—and it was going well. The teachers were very helpful and sup-

○°○
○

parenting bubble ALERT!

Home-schooling

I'm sure there are instances in which home-schooling feels necessary: where the schools are intractably horrid, where moving isn't an option, where you're an insane religious zealot who thinks bigoted brain-washing benefits kids. But you don't "home dentist" or "home neurologist" your child, do you? Why? Because when you're not expert in something having to do with their welfare, it's best to rely on the skills of trained professionals. Now, it may come as a surprise to you, but most teachers are trained professionals with years of schooling and experience. Ask yourself, What is it about the level of disrespect for the job of teaching that makes so many people assume that they could do it better?

portive, and she'd acclimated readily. "In fact, she hadn't cried at drop-off since the first week. Until the past few days, while I've been gone. I'm not sure what happened, but clearly Miguel fucked something up."

I tried to unpack this. "Has he taken her to school before?"

"Yes, of course. He came on her first day and maybe some other times as well. But usually he picks up; and I drop off. It's on my way to work. Why?"

"Well, it could be as simple as that." I explained. As grown-ups, we imagine that kids see all familiar adults, particularly their primary caregivers, as interchangeable. "But a switch like having another parent take them to school can be a big adjustment to a young child, especially if it's a break with their routine. They rely on the structure of the familiar to help them deal with all the change that's constantly going on around them."

Clarisse nodded and threw back her beer. "I suppose."

I pursed my lips. She seemed distracted. ". . . What? There's something else?"

"It's nothing, really. The whole situation with her falling apart at drop-off just made me think of something. But it's kind of unrelated."

"I'm sure it's related."

"It is."

"So tell me."

"It's going to sound stupid. And narcissistic." She opened a fresh beer. "Okay. Fine. I guess I just wonder . . . Why she doesn't ever cry when I say good-bye anymore? Even just a little. It makes me feel . . . unloved."

Though it was probably just the alcohol talking, I was still touched that my friend revealed this base emotion to me—one that many parents surely feel but are too proud to admit. I had to come up with a good response. "It's not a reflection of how much she loves or misses you," I said. "Rest assured, she loves you. You're her mom. But, as I'm sure I've said a million times before, kids are comforted by routines. Since she's been through the drop-off routine enough times with you, she feels secure in the fact you'll come back, and so separation is no longer problematic for her. It's not that she doesn't love you. It's that she feels safe. It's a good thing."

This explanation seemed to work. Clarisse nodded. "That makes sense."

"Anyway, you should watch what you wish for. You're likely to be more than fulfilled on the bawling front soon enough."

"What do you mean?"

I explained that kids' anticipation about starting school can often help them warm to it quickly, especially at first. "But like in a marriage, the hard part comes once the honeymoon ends and they begin to realize that this isn't just a new, exciting experience, but one that'll be going on regularly for the rest of their life." Once habituation sets in—usually between three weeks and three months into the year—issues often begin to arise.

"Great," Clarisse said. "So what should I expect, lunch-box throwing? Truancy?"

I smiled. "Well, kids don't have the same ability to deal with cause and effect that we do, so the issues that pop up won't necessarily be around school. They could be around things like toileting or bedtime. By the same token, if she does scream and yell at drop-off time, it doesn't mean that she hates school or that you're a bad parent—just like it doesn't mean you hate your kid or you're a bad parent if, three weeks after they're born, you start crying and wondering if you've made a huge mistake. It just means that she's adjusting to large-scale, long-term change."

"So . . . you don't think I made the wrong choice? You don't think it has anything to do with the school?"

"I doubt it. I was only there that one time, but they seemed pretty right-on." I nodded. "Did Miguel give you any sense of how they dealt with things today?"

"He said they were pretty matter-of-fact. He hugged her, they hugged her, and they all reminded her that he'd be back at the end of the day. Then they had him wave good-bye and ushered him out. Apparently she stopped crying right after he left."

"Sounds like they have the right idea."

"Well, how did you handle things like this at your school?" she asked. "The whole start of the year? Helping kids feel comfortable?"

I smiled. "We did things a little differently from most places. We took a very long-term approach. It was a lot of work."

"Well . . . Is it top secret or something?"

"No. It's just . . . very involved. And it's sort of ideal—a product of my compulsion—so I don't want you to feel bad if Katia's school doesn't do the same things."

"I've got time. And a heart of coal. You know that. So spill."

I spilled. We started working with the incoming class the spring before they started school. As soon as I'd made my admissions decisions and people had put down their enrollment deposits, we hosted a getting-to-know-you event at the school for all the incoming families. This gave the kids a chance to see the space and meet the staff again—they'd all come for a visit/observation as part of the admissions process—and it allowed them to meet the other newbies in their class. It also gave the new parents a chance to connect with the teachers and each other, as well as with some of the returning moms and dads, who attended to help explain things from a familial perspective.

Following this, during the summer, I would go on a "home visit" to each of the incoming kids' houses. This was literally just what it sounds like, an appointment where I would stop by their place to talk to the family and answer questions. This gave the kids and their parents the opportunity to meet me on their home turf, helping to develop trust and bridge the home–school divide—key to developing a positive working relationship. It also allowed me to see who the parents were as people and what the kid's home life was like—the kinds of rules and structure they lived with—so I could bring this back to my staff and contextualize each kid's situation. Home visits also sent the important message to the child that I was a safe and familiar person—I'd been invited over to their house. But perhaps most important, they gave me a chance to bond with the kid and provided something concrete to draw on when they walked through the door on the first day of school. *Remember me?* I could ask. *Remember when I came to your house?*

Parents would often try to show off during these visits, having their kid recite the ABCs or some such shtick, so I always made sure to structure the visit so that it ended with my hanging out with the child alone. This was a way of counteracting parental anxiety or pressure, letting the kid know that I was much more interested in them and their stuff than whatever tricks their parents had trained them to perform. It was also a trust exercise for the parents: I was going to be with their kid all the time come fall; if they didn't trust me to hang out with them alone for ten minutes, our relationship wasn't going to work very well. We usually ended up sitting in the kid's room, reading a book.

Once the school year started, we had what we called a "slow start" policy for the new kids. The first few days were half days, and parents were asked to arrange things so that someone—preferably whoever would generally be handling drop-off—was available for this entire time. To help kids adjust to the idea that their parent would leave but would always return, parents were asked to hang around the classroom and then say good-bye and depart for increasingly longer stretches of time. By the end of the first week, most kids (and most parents) were usually ready to separate for the whole day.

Of course, like anything with young children, this process took patience and follow-through to function properly. Most parents were good about adhering to our strategies—waiting to separate until we all felt their child was ready to handle it—and while the process could be arduous at times, the investment up front paid off in the long run. By working through separation anxiety while it was happening, we helped kids and parents figure out how to feel fully secure and confident about coming to school. But there were always a few folks who tried to drop and ditch, sneaking out on the first day when their kid wasn't looking, in the hope of avoiding confrontation. Their child might not notice at first, offering short-term success. But when they did, it always resulted in their feeling panicked and abandoned, setting a poor course for drop-off time in the future, and for how these families connected with the school in general.

"Like almost everything with young kids," I said, getting a bit preachy, "these initial experiences set their course and become their templates. With drop-off time, and separation, it's all about developing trust between parent and child."

Clarisse slammed her hand on the table. "Well, then we're definitely going back to my dropping her off," she said. "*I* want to be the one she trusts. *Me*. She's not going to run to her dad when she gets her period or when some boy's trying to get into her pants. If I have another one and it's a boy, *he* can handle *that*." She raised her beer bottle in a toast and I clinked it with mine. "Well, this has been great. Thanks for talking me down." Clarisse threw some meat onto the grill in the middle of the table. "Now I have just one more question, and then we can go back to being normal friends. Okay?"

I nodded.

"All right. Here it is," Clarisse slurred. "How do you get a kid to tell you what they did in school that day? I try with Katia all the time, but whenever I do, she just looks at me like I'm asking her to recite the tax code or something."

"Well, how do you ask?" I said.

"I don't know." She shrugged. "Something like '*What'd you do in school today?*' "

I gave Clarisse my standard spiel, telling her to grasp on to specifics, to move from the concrete to the abstract, and not to limit her drive for information by only asking questions that have right or wrong or one-word answers.

She looked unconvinced. "I've tried all that. At the school, they even post a Daily News sheet that outlines the activities they did that day, along with a running list of recommended questions. It doesn't work."

I nodded. "All I can say is, keep trying."

"I have. It's not working." She squinted her eyes, and a look of triumph overcame her. "You don't have an answer, do you? I finally stumped the expert!"

"Is *that* your goal? Christ, I can't believe how competitive you are." I shook my head. "Anyway, I hate to disappoint you, but I *do* have an answer." I told her that she had to recognize that school is frequently a young child's first experience having something that is totally their own and that they often

parenting bubble ALERT!

Q: What Did You Do in School Today? A: Nothing

It is important to remember that kids' mental processing skills are very different from ours, especially in terms of memory and recall. They live in the concrete and the present tense. The past—even the recent past—is neither of these things. So a question like "What did you do in school today?" is as abstract and annoying to a child as someone's asking you "What's it's like in America?" An entire school day entails far too many overlapping segments for a young child to process at once and lacks the tangible footholds they need in order to craft a response. You need to be much more specific. Familiarize yourself with their classroom: its occupants, materials, and routines. That way, if you discover that there's a book read every day at story time, you can ask solid questions like "What was the book at story time today?" and "What were the characters in that book?" You can then use this as "scaffolding" to move into abstractions such as "What did you like about the story?" or "What was good about those parts?" Once you've got your child rooted and warmed up, ask them to retell things—events, stories, responses. This is a great way to help them develop their sense of narrative and create templates for future recall.

want to relish these experiences and keep them to themselves. "This can change, and kids who are mum at first can find ways to open up. But all kids need and deserve things that are private from their parents."

Clarisse nodded and seemed to be taking this in. But then she shook her head. "Not my kid," she said.

GUG'S TIPS FOR HANDLING:

Starting School

Starting school is a big change—for kids as well as for parents—and so it's best to plan on breaking the process down and handling it in stages. Here are some of the key steps you'll need to take.

- *Lay the Groundwork:* Kids' issues with starting school are often not about fear of schools but rather anxiety regarding the unknown. If you gently help your child become familiar with what to expect from this new experience, these feelings will diminish. Remember, *be concrete;* real-life examples are needed in order to make it real for kids. Also remember, kids don't develop linearly—mastering one thing fully, and then moving on to the next. They tend to bounce around a bit. Therefore, ideas and suggestions from prior stages may need to be continued throughout the prep process.

  Stage 1 (3–5 months out): Casually bring up the idea of their starting school, but place it *firmly* and *concretely* in the future (*"You'll start in September; after the summer; when you turn three"*). Walk or drive by their school building and point it out. Make note of other kids your child knows who are already going to school and/or who will be starting at the same time and/or same school as them.

  Stage 2 (1–3 months out): Tell your child what they'll be doing at school. Describe the events and routines of the school day. Be sure to note that you'll be dropping them off and won't be present—but don't forget to mention that you'll return to pick them up. Try to arrange a visit to the classroom.

  Stage 3 (2–4 weeks out): Get your child directly involved. Let them choose a lunch box and backpack. Practice walking/driving to the school and noting things on your route. Make a countdown calendar and let them cross off the days. Create bedtime and morning routines (see below).

- *Create Routines:* Develop and implement functional bedtime and morning routines *at least a week or two before your child's start date.* The first day of school is hard enough. Adding a bunch of new items to your agenda on that day will virtually guarantee that your kid will be in hysterics before you leave the house. If your child already has a stable and familiar structure to follow on their first day, they'll feel comforted and prepared. It will also be easier for them to add "go to school" to this existing pattern.

- *Take It Slow:* Ask the school *in advance* about its plan for helping you and your child through this transition. This is a big step—sometimes bigger for parents than kids. I personally don't think cold turkey is the best practice, but every school handles things differently, so if they say, "We just have you drop him at the door," you may want to redouble your efforts with respect to the points above.

- *Expect Bumps:* Be prepared for crying. Lots of crying. It may not happen on the first day or during the first few weeks. It may not happen to your child at all—*you* may be the one in tears. But fallout from this separation is normal. Remember to think nonlinearly. Effects or regression may pop up in places other than those having to do directly with school. *Don't* shift your standards in response ("You can wear diapers again"). *Do* be understanding ("I see you had another accident. Let's work together to think of some ways to help remind you to use the bathroom").

- *Try a Transitional Object:* One way to help ease the pain of separation is to let your child bring something of theirs or yours with them to school. A transitional object like this can give kids something concrete on which to ground their anxiety, thus dissipating it. This item should be as inconspicuous as possible: a key to your house, a tiny toy, a pebble from your yard. Your child can keep it in their pocket or cubby and visit it—but just when they're feeling sad. (You don't want them to become that weird kid with the rock.)

- *Respect Your Child's World:* School is a new realm for your child and is often the first one that will exist outside of your direct supervision. If you want to know what's going on there, you need to be informed and engaged. But you also need to respect your child's developmental need to create a world and sense of self that's separate from you. Getting your child to talk about school, and linking school and home, are good ways of deepening their experiences and education. But be aware that they're not going to want to tell you everything, and they shouldn't have to.

- *Don't Feel Guilty:* Change can be challenging and difficult. But you are entitled to work and live your life, and a quality school is a vital and important place for young kids. If you're consistent, understanding, and involved—and you've done *everything I say*—your child will probably thrive there.

SAY "UNCLE!"

12.
Boob Tubes
Consuming Media

TAL AND I didn't buy any Christmas presents for our nieces. We're not total curmudgeons. We're just not all that enamored with the holiday season: its false cheer, its enforced commerce, Tal's mom's reindeer appliqué sweaters. We're fans of any excuse to tipple back a few, so we appreciate all the parties, but that's about the extent of our joyfulness. Still, I think that kids expect to find gifts from their uncles under the tree, especially if said uncles are going to be there in person. Since I'd been consulting on some big kids' TV projects that year, I had piles of sample DVDs lying around the house, containing about a hundred episodes of some of the most popular shows on the air. Thinking of the girls, I threw these in a shopping bag just before we headed out the door.

Once we arrived at Tal's parents' place, we wrapped a stack of discs up for each of our nieces. Because of my expertise in child development and my background as an educator, many of the media projects I work on focus on early childhood educational properties: shows, Web sites, video games, or toys that are intended to achieve instructional outcomes with kids age two to six. Now, I don't have a totally rigid moral compass when it comes to my consulting practice—for example, I sometimes take on jobs whose sole intent is to figure out how to sell kids more junk food—but in working in the field for nearly ten years, I've certainly developed the ability to discern quality from crap, and I'm not about to give my young relatives anything I feel is inappropriate. I also knew for a fact that all these girls watched TV. So while Lizzie and her daughter Violet seemed very appreciative when they opened their box, I was quite surprised at the reaction of my sister-in-law Cindy.

"*The World's Tiniest Dog*?" she said in horror, as if I'd just given the girls a copy of *Teen Anal IV*. "*I the Spy*?" She inspected the cases. "What channel are these on?"

"I think it's Playboy," I said brightly. "But it all airs before midnight, so I guess it's officially part of Playboy Jr., their kids' network." Cindy did not look amused. "Kidding," I said. I told her the name of the actual channel, a wildly popular media outlet with some highly rated preschool programming. They had a Ph.D.-level consultant on staff whose work I very much respected, and they were top of mind for parents whenever educational TV was mentioned. Plus, *I* had elected to give the shows to the girls, which seemed like the best possible endorsement. Cindy worked for a big dental HMO. If I wanted information on what kind of veneers to have installed, I'd trust her recommendation implicitly.

Cindy dropped the discs back in the box and gave it a half shove in my direction. She glanced dismissively at Lizzie, whom she often treated as a combatant in terms of their approach to parenting "Well, I don't know about you and Violet," she said. "But *we* don't watch that channel," she said. "We only watch documentaries and PBS."

I knew for a fact that this wasn't true. Since I started working in

Media Posturing

In interviewing many thousands of parents and children about what, when, and how often they watch TV, I have come to the conclusion that just about everyone in America lies about their media consumption. And no one lies more than parents of young kids. I've literally talked to parents who tell me their kid watches nothing but a half hour of *Sesame Street* each week, and then had their child come in and spell out a viewing schedule that rivals the workweek of a Malaysian sweatshop employee, listing their favorite shows as *CSI*, *The Real World*, and *Desperate Housewives*. I think parents *should* be embarrassed about letting their kids watch programming like this and about the fact that the average American child spends more hours in front of the TV than they do attending school. But the solution to this situation isn't to pull a Dubyah and pretend it isn't happening; it's to pretend you're the grown-up and take charge of making change.

kids' media, I've made a point of asking just about every child I come across what they watch, listen to, and log on to. It's not only a means of connecting with them, it helps me to remain au courant. I've also found that when kids find out that I helped make some of their favorite movies, sites, and shows, they have a tendency to like me more. Based in part on these desperate needs, I'd had an extended conversation with Brooke and Daphne just the day before, in which it became clear that their exposure was far greater than Cindy claimed.

Now, I've learned that there are other viable explanations for this disparity: kids partake of things at friends' houses that they're not allowed at home; they create entire narratives for stuff they've only glimpsed in ads; they even sometimes realize an awareness of properties they've never actually seen, tapping into a shadowy underground collective I call the Preschool Osmotic Unconscious. But these types of exposure, while strangely meaningful and potent for young kids, usually lack a certain depth: they're limited to yielding an understanding only of basic elements like character ("There's a green one and a purple one") and characterization ("The green one is good, and the purple one is bad"). Brooke and Daphne's knowledge ran much deeper than this.

The strange thing about all of my sister-in-law's posturing was that it didn't seem to have much of a point—unless you count trying to make Lizzie and Violet feel badly about their own media habits. So far as I can tell, this seems to be the sole intent of this kind of soapboxing—a behavior I believe speaks volumes about the muddled relationship we have with media in our culture. We are endless consumers of it, and our consumption feeds on itself (witness the popularity of media that solely covers media). Now that the means of production and distribution are much more widely accessible, we're even obsessed with creating our own. One would think that with its pervasive presence, we'd be more open about our media diets. But then again, we're a country full of young drug addicts and pregnant teens that's stuck on policies like Just Say No and Abstinence Only—despite the fact that every study in the world has shown that this kind of denial is not only ineffective but counterproductive—so I guess the idea of our putting our heads in the sand about anything shouldn't really come as a surprise.

Maybe openness isn't our thing nationally, but it's my thing in this book. So I'm going to come right out and say it: I'm not opposed to children's media. I'm not even opposed, as some purported experts have been, to children's media for kids under the age of two. This doesn't mean I advocate unlimited or unsupervised exposure. *I don't even advocate exposure at all*—it's certainly not a necessity. But I don't think it's healthy for parents to *pretend* that kids' media doesn't exist or that *their* kid doesn't watch or isn't affected by it. Taking this position just excuses you from educating your child on how to deal with media in a savvy and intelligent way—what we call media literacy. Again, the sex-ed paradigm is of use: even if you don't think your teenager is having intercourse right now, even if you'd like to hope or pretend that they're never going to have it, do you think it serves their interests to deny them the basic understanding of how it works and works on them? Having spent many years on the front lines in

One Tiny *GUG* Minute On: Kids' Media Learning

Studies have shown that children's media can help kids learn specific information (recognizing letters, numbers, shapes, and colors). In my work as a researcher, I've also seen indicators of the following.

- Watching and discussing videos of familiar stories can help kids to better understand how written narratives work—an important emergent literacy skill.

- Playing video games can provide kids with templates for the further exploration of subjects that interest them: the ability to "drill down" to uncover more about something.

- Exposure to pro-social messages embedded in media narratives can help kids deal with sensitive issues like breaking down cultural stereotypes.

- Music- and movement-based content can encourage kids to participate in physical activity.

creating media for young kids, I can tell you with unguarded certainty that it's presence isn't diminishing.

I think age-appropriate media is perfectly acceptable, *with supervision, and in moderation.* Having designed, fielded, and interpreted scientific studies about the impact of media on children's development, I can even say with confidence that quality educational media can be good for kids. This doesn't mean that the more media your child consumes the smarter they'll end up or that if you plop them in front of the TV all day, they're going to become Nobel laureates. My rule of thumb for kids' media is to follow the directions on chewable vitamins: one daily dose (administered under your direct supervision) has the potential to be worthwhile; two probably offers no ancillary benefits; and after that it just runs right out of them.

Again, I'm not in any way advocating constant or unsupervised media viewing, and I think that the benefits of passive exposure (like the craze of playing Mozart to your baby) are likely nil. I also feel it's acceptable to create media-free zones in the life of your young child. When I was running a preschool, we didn't have computers in the classrooms, we didn't even have a TV or a means to screen videos. In fact, our most advanced media system was an old turntable on which I'd play records that I'd buy up in the Catskills: Duke Ellington, Frank Sinatra, Tito Puente, Roberta Flack. But we made visits to the public library every Friday to check out its children's literature-to-film series. It got the kids into the library. It connected them with the stories and books featured in the movies. And, to be perfectly honest, it was a fun and exciting way to give everyone a release at the week's end.

This brings up another important function of children's media: providing kids with an opportunity to take a break and be entertained. Not all media are overtly, or even covertly, educational. There's plenty of age-appropriate content out there, which—like ice cream or candy—isn't *good* for kids per se, but can serve as a treat and have little negative impact *when consumed in moderation.* Kids today have busy schedules, and growing up is hard work. When I was in grad school, someone told me that we use fewer calories watching TV than we do when we sleep. I'm not sure if this is true, but I believe that kids should be allowed to veg out like this now and again. Isn't that part of why *we* watch TV, listen to music, and surf the Web? Isn't admitting this healthier than pretending we're only in it to expand our cultural understanding?

Of course, these opportunities, like junk food, need to be dished out in small doses. And guess whose job it is to create the rules and practical routines to govern this? *Yours!* Your kid is not capable of regulating their media consumption any more than they're capable of deciding their own bedtime, cooking a healthy meal, or balancing a checkbook. Some kids are temperamentally better at self-regulating than others, and I've met plenty of kids who aren't

CHECK, PLEASE

YOUR HANDY GUG CHECKLIST FOR:

Media Diets

The most important thing you can do to help your child develop a balanced relationship with media is to ensure that they have clear limits placed on how, when, and what media they consume, and a rational and age-appropriate understanding of why these limits exist. (It also helps if you model balanced and self-regulating behaviors yourself.) This is what people mean when they talk about making kids media literate: giving them the ability to understand how media works and providing them with tools to examine its messages and methods so that they can control its impact on them instead of the other way around. Your proscriptions and rules teach your child what is and is not appropriate and acceptable. If you abdicate this responsibility, you're letting the media police itself. Is this really the cop you'd hire? Here are some steps you can take.

○ Only allow your child to partake of media for a set amount of time each week, say, one hour a day.

○ Only allow them to watch at certain prescribed times: in the morning, after school, before bed.

○ Only allow them to watch if they've completed the full set of other more relevant tasks, like chores, getting dressed, eating a healthy meal, etc.

○ Be sure to balance media consumption with other, more active forms of entertainment (both physically and mentally), such as playing outdoors, making things, reading/being read to, and dramatic play.

○ Only allow your child to engage with media properties you've prescreened and deemed acceptable.

○ Watch along with your child when possible: ask questions, interact, point out tactics, raise concerns.

○ Alert your child to the distinctions between media and real life.

○ Alert your child to the distinctions between media and advertising.

interested in media at all. But while I recognize that setting media intake limits for your child can be a challenge, please note that *all of these devices have an on and off switch, while being a parent does not.*

We have a big systemic problem in this country in terms of addressing public health issues: we either rely on market solutions—hoping that panaceas like "consumer choice" will solve epidemics like obesity on their own—or we simply ignore them and do nothing. I strongly believe that there should be a targeted, federally funded initiative to help families learn how to create a healthy balance in their child's intake of things like food, activities, and media. But I also think that health care, affordable housing, child care, and a quality education should be rights and not privileges. Since we're not anywhere near there in this country (at least not yet), as a parent you have a responsibility to seek out information on these subjects and pass it along to your child. Remember, the ultimate goal is to shift regulating responsibility onto your kid, so you don't just want to act as a cop; you want to educate them, set up expectations, and help them find their own center. Like so many other things with young kids, this is about *you* providing the limits needed to teach *them* self-control, so they can develop a healthy sense of balance.

I think of these rules whenever the issue of kids and media comes up: during talks with friends and family, when I'm moderating focus groups with parents, when I'm interviewing kids about what they watch and play with. We all know just how seductive media and media devices are. If this wasn't the case, a million comics wouldn't still be trying to make their careers on jokes about people using cell phones in inappropriate places, and my friend Staffan wouldn't be spending our entire lunch halfheartedly nodding at my stories, while pretending that he's not obsessively checking his BlackBerry. It therefore shouldn't be surprising that if you bookmark Barbie.com for your four-year-old, place a satellite-enabled TV in the room of your six-year-old, or buy your eleven-year-old a Sidekick—*and fail to provide some education on etiquette and some limits on usage*—that they should fall into an unseemly spiral.

I thought of all of this as our nieces finished flipping through the videos I gave them that Christmas. It should be noted that they quickly moved on to other, more dynamic gifts—remote-controlled talking bunnies, one-billion-piece bead-stringing kits, the omnipresent and compulsively diminutive world of Polly Pocket! But my sister-in-law Cindy was nothing if not tenacious, and (like me) loved to grind an ax, and so she kept puckishly wrenching the conversation back to the DVDs. For example:

TAL: You know who Sophia Bush is. She was in that remake of *The Hitcher.*

CINDY: Oh, right, isn't that one of the films that you just gave my daughters?

And

TAL'S MOM: I saw this graphic documentary the other day on our use of torture in Iraq. It was very upsetting.

CINDY: I'll have to check that out. I think it's in the box of movies that Brett gave to the girls.

And

BRETT: Our neighbor recently ran into an escaped horse with his car. Its head burst through the windshield, and it bled all over the place.

CINDY: That's awful. I guess it's lucky he had his video camera with him so he could film the accident and you could give a copy to Brooke and Daphne.

Given the grotesque number of presents they each received, you wouldn't imagine that Christmas morning would wind down with our nieces embroiled in an all-out fight over who got more/better/prettier gifts, but it did. (You see why I hate the holidays?) The situation was remedied by our annual hike in the Blue Ridge Mountains. Since our earth is heating up alarmingly, the weather was sunny and in the sixties, and the usually windswept walk was eerily comfortable. The girls were excellent hikers and led the way in both directions. Unfortunately, this exertion had the side effect of exhausting their strategic energy reserves, and the kids-only early-dinner seating we held in the hope of staving off any crankiness abruptly ended in a whiny meltdown.

By this point, my favorite part of Christmas had finally begun—the annual homemade, bourbon-fueled eggnog chug-off—and while the nieces' irritability wasn't too extreme, the grown-up's patience and ability for dealing with them was limited by a desire to stay close to the punch bowl so as not to miss out on the limited supply. Tal's sister Lizzie came to the rescue, suggesting that the girls take a bath together and then hold a slumber party in the den. Lizzie had a remarkable aptitude for instigating while appearing to placate, especially when it came to her rivalry with Cindy, and so it wasn't surprising so much as deliciously horrifying when she turned to the girls and said saccharinely, "Maybe you'd like to watch some of the DVDs the Uncles gave you?"

Our nieces leapt at the opportunity, and I leapt out of the room, not wanting to witness the ensuing fireworks. But, strangely, everything seemed to progress without incident or indictment. The moms took the girls upstairs, I heard the water running and draining, and before I could even finish my lucid dissection of *The Passion of the Christ* (which I, quite stridently, had not seen) with Tal's dad, both Cindy and Lizzie were back downstairs. My glass was empty, and I had already laid down the one trump card a Jewish in-law has with a Christian family—I called the movie anti-Semitic. Having thus brought the conversation with my father-in-law to an abrupt end, I excused myself and joined the rest of the family in the kitchen. Tal was helping his mom make dessert, but everyone else was gathered around the punch bowl, and as I heard the familiar sound of the scraping of the bottom of the barrel, I muscled my way in, hoping to squeeze out a last ration. Sadly, there were too many people queued up in front of me. My share of the nog would be naught. I blamed *The Passion of the Christ*. I blamed Jesus. But channeling my frustration into provocation, I turned to the gloatingly full-glassed Lizzie. "Sounds like it's going pretty smoothly up there," I said.

She nodded and passed the ladle to Cindy. "Yeah. Violet told me to tell you that she loves those shows, especially *The World's Tiniest Dog*."

"That's great." I stared, nearly salivating, as Cindy dribbled the final scoop into her cup. "So . . . what are Brooke and Daphne doing? Reading the encyclopedia? Listening to Bible stories on your iPod?"

"Fuck no. They're in there watching." She smiled. "It's Christmas. We all deserve a break. Plus, I wait all year for Lizzie's eggnog." She triumphantly dropped the ladle into the empty bowl. "You're out of your mind if you think I'm going to stay up there fighting to get my girls to bed while y'all are down here drinking it."

Though it wasn't at all comforting, the only thing I could think to say was, "Touché."

GUG'S TIPS FOR HANDLING:

Kids' Media

Media are pervasive and becoming increasingly more so—advertisements recently blared at me from the handle of the gas pump as I inserted it into my tank. So you need to provide your kids with the tools they'll need to begin their lifelong engagement with it. Try some of these tips at the very least.

- **Test Drive:** Young kids should never be set free on any media property on their own. You wouldn't send your kid to a school or leave them with a babysitter without a proper interview, would you? Media will likely play as large a role—if not larger—in your child's life, so make sure they get your proper attention. Remember, during their initial forays into media, your kid will need your help: to select the channel, create the bookmark, load the DVD, etc. Take advantage of this role as gatekeeper to enforce your will and to make your expectations known.

- **America's Next Top Model:** When you're screening media with your kid, be sure to let them know what you like and what you don't, and why. Modeling a critical perspective on media—that it's a topic open for discussion—helps your child to develop skills they'll need to become media literate.

- **Co-View:** You don't have to watch, surf, play, or listen to every thing your child does. (Thank god!) But being present and asking questions about what they're experiencing has been proven to deepen what your kid can learn from media. Simple questions are a good place to start ("Which of those dragons is the blue one?"), but try to aim for more complex concepts like problem solving and prediction ("How are they going to get out of there?" "What do you think is going to happen next?"). These are key narrative comprehension skills, important for developing literacy. Co-viewing also gives you the added bonus of knowing what's going on in the worlds your child is exploring, thus providing you with the means to respond to, extend, or counter the messages included there.

- *Commercialus Interruptus:* This may come as a surprise to you, but kids do not innately know the difference between a program/game/ Web site and the advertising that is included in or surrounds these things. Pointing this out, and explaining what it's for—to try to get you to buy stuff—is a key step in helping your child understand media's intent and messages. It will also help limit those "I want a Mini-Micro-Robots Morphology Lab!" breakdowns at the department store.

- *Portion Control:* Your child is not capable of regulating their media diet on their own. You must take charge of it, or it will more than likely take charge of you and them. Decide when, what, where, and how much media they can consume. Create reasonable limits, explain them clearly, expect your child to follow them, and create and execute repercussions if they don't.

- *Keep a Balance:* You've seen the outdoors, right? It's the stuff on the other side of your windows. Tell your child to go out and run around in it on a regular basis. Better yet, go out and run around in it yourself. There is no better way to get your child to understand the importance of exercise than demonstrating the key role it plays in your own life. And don't forget about imaginative play, reading books, and having conversations. These are all important alternatives to endless media consumption.

SAY "UNCLE!"

Snappy Answers to Common Problems

THOUGH I BELIEVE I've covered some of the most pressing and wide-ranging themes in early childhood, I recognize that it's often the smaller and more pointed issues that truly rattle and embarrass parents. For this reason, I've included a few handfuls of such topics in this quick-reference guide. Please note that the inclusion of these subjects here is meant to underscore the *extremely common* nature of their incidence, and to help you realize that *your child is not the first one to exhibit these behaviors.* Also note that just because your child does these things once, and you respond according to my directions, it does not guarantee that they won't repeat the behavior. Like I've said before, making change takes time. You may therefore want to dog-ear these pages so you can reference them in the future when your child does the same thing again.

ANNOYING BEHAVIOR

Young children have a seemingly limitless ability to seek out and execute actions that get on the nerves of the adults around them: endlessly spinning in their chair, splashing water out of the tub, pushing the braying horse-noise button on their Big Red Barn talking picture book. Most of these actions aren't innately unsafe or destructive, but that doesn't make them any less irksome. If you try to fight or control each one, though, you're going to exhaust yourself and/or become a tyrant. My advice is therefore to ignore or rationalize whatever minor issues you can (the bathroom is a waterproof room and is thus made to be splashed in). If you want to put the kibosh on something, you should use the EAR method (see chapter 6). But for smaller issues, you can also try the COO: the Co-Option Option. A big part of the fun your child derives from their annoying behaviors comes from bothering you and/or resisting your will. If you remove these elements from the equation, their interest will diminish. The trick is to provide boundaries and parameters for your surrender: tell your child they can perform the annoying action a set number of times ("You can push the horse-noise button twenty times; I'll count with you") or for a certain duration ("You can spin in that chair for one minute straight; I'll time you"). Just be sure to let them know that after this quota is up, they'll need to stop and move on ("Once your minute of spinning is over, you need to sit steady and eat your lunch"). And provide repercussions if they don't ("Or I'll take the spinning chair away and get a hard chair for you to sit in"). COOing not only makes you a party to their fun, it helps you to see how silly it is to get worked up over insignificant irritants. Plus, it actually works.

BITING

Parents feel a sense of utter horror when their child bites someone, likely because there's something about this act that peels away our alleged sophistication and superiority and reveals our true nature. It bites! It's an animal! In reality, biting is very common in kids. It usually happens when a child is on a developmental cusp, and they find themselves overwhelmed by a social situation and without access to appropriate linguistic means to respond appropriately—literally when they're *at a loss for words*. Biting children usually don't intend harm. It's just the product of frustration and instinct. As usual, it's your response that creates meaning for them. All too often, however, a parent's inordinate shock and dismay can work against them, serving to reinforce this behavior instead of inhibiting it. (Kids are drawn to anything that generates a strong reaction.) Obviously, biting is not acceptable and should be prohibited, but if it does happen, try to divest from your gut terror and discuss it calmly and with the explicit provision of more appropriate alternatives. And don't forget to clean the bitee's wound with mild soap and cool water, particularly if your little Miss Chompers has broken the skin. Also, know that most kids bite only once or twice in their lives, so don't extrapolate from the first nip to a lifetime of vampirism or cannibalism.

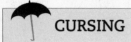

CURSING

Try as you may to avoid using what my third-grade teacher called a garbage mouth in front of your young child, they're inevitably going to be exposed to the wonders of four-letter words—by you, by their peers, by watching cable with the sitter. Swearing is an expressive and exciting part of our language. I love to curse when the situation demands it—and sometimes when it doesn't. Perhaps you do too. But young kids don't have our contextual understanding of proper or improper usage, so when they try cursing (like with most other things they do) they're attempting to figure out the boundaries of propriety and acceptability. It's your job to provide these parameters. Probably more than once. I personally have much less trouble with young kids swearing than I do with them engaging in violent play, so long as they do it properly and without intending harm to others. Calling another a child "asshole" when they cut the line for the slide is unacceptable. But I see no problem with a child screaming "Shit!" when they drop a block on their toe. You may feel differently, however. So when your kid tries out a new curse word, let them know your stance. If you think it's not appropriate, say so. If you think it's okay at home but not at school, make that rule. But keep your invocations calm and straightforward, and then let it lie. If you lose your mind every time they curse, they're going to quickly learn that this is an excellent way to get a rise out of you, and this will only encourage them to do it more. (And please, no soaping out their mouths. That is so retro and metaphorical, neither of which means anything to a young kid.) If you've already dug yourself into this hole or find they're cursing to accomplish this end, your best bet is to calmly tell them once that it's inappropriate and then ignore it. It may take a while, but I fucking swear it will go away.

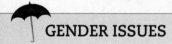

GENDER ISSUES

While hummingbirds naturally gravitate toward the color red, and there's some evidence that bees are provoked by large black objects (they remind them of bears coming to steal their honey) I've not seen any studies proving that human newborns are hardwired by gender to connect with either pink or blue. And contrary to the scuttlebutt in the playground, all boys are not inherently drawn to violence and domination, and girls to secretarial skills. This gendering of colors, behaviors, and nearly everything else is accomplished mainly through a million subtle and not-so-subtle cues that kids begin receiving even before they're born. So if your boy child is overly aggressive, or your daughter is unable to leave the house without spending two hours getting her face together, it's likely at least in part your fault. I'm all for letting kids try on gender stereotypes—they need to do this in order to make sense of their place in the world around them—so I think it's fine for girls to fall deeply in love with their hairbrush or for boys to want to be a heroic (and swarthy) fireman when they grow up. But I'm asking you to be aware of how all this plays out and not to be any more lenient of debilitating or inappropriate behaviors (the need to wear high heels to the playground, the monomaniacal drive to always be first) based on their adherence with notions of "traditional" gender roles. I'm also vehemently against forcing any kid to adhere to these roles: convincing a girl to wear a skirt when she prefers a tool belt; discouraging a boy from going to gymnastics camp. My grandma Micky tried desperately to convince my mother not to buy me a G.I. Joe doll, claiming it would make me queer. Tal's dad tried to warn his mom off taking him to see *Gone with the Wind* for the same reason. But that was in back in the Dark Ages of the 1970s. Parents' big motivations in pushing their kids to conform to conventional gendered behavior—that they'll otherwise turn out either "weird" or gay—have no place in our modern understanding of gender or sexuality. Male dolls and classic cinema aside, your kids are born innately gay or weird, and it's your *job* to be proud of them however they turn out.

LYING

Most young kids have difficulty distinguishing between fantasy and reality when they're relating information. Part of this is because it's hard for them to accurately recall anything beyond the proximal and present tense. Part of it is because they're constantly being exposed to a torrent of new ideas and their tiny brains are short-circuited by their efforts to incorporate it all. And part of it is because they're innately evil and are the mouthpieces of the devil. Obviously, you should help them learn to understand the distinction between truth and invention—you can point out concrete examples in books or movies or in their lives. But when you're grilling them about how their Polly Pocket! Disco Roller Rink ended up under the bathroom sink the previous week, their confessions shouldn't be held to the same standards as a defendant in a criminal trial. What we think of as "lying" often reflects a child's best efforts—given their limited abilities—to reconstruct a past event, to create a comprehensible solution for an occurrence whose causality they don't actually understand, or simply to tell us what they believe we want to hear. In these cases, focus on the action you want them to accomplish ("Put your toys away when you're done with them") rather than the confounding pathway leading up to it, and then move on.

In the rare instances when you're forced to determine culpability regarding an action you think your young child may have taken, do everyone a favor and don't bother with questions to which you already know the answer. ("Who drew this backward yellow *E* on the dining-room wall?") Just spell out the situation and the solution for them. (*"Crayons are to be used on paper only. I'm going to get a rag so you can help me clean this up."*) If your child suspects you're so dumb you can't tell when they're the culprit, they're sure to feel that you won't be able to detect a lie. If, however, you let them think you're omnipotent and all-knowing, it's less likely they'll see the value of attempting to hide the truth in the first place.

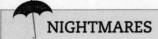

NIGHTMARES

Nightmares are frightening to adults, so you can imagine what they must be like to little kids who lack our (alleged) ability to differentiate between fantasy and reality. When a child has a bad dream, they need and deserve to be comforted. But we all also need and deserve boundaries and privacy. In responding to a child's nightmare, it's certainly easier to just let them crawl into bed with you. But I hope that if you've learned anything from reading this book, it's that the easiest choice isn't necessarily the right one. Kids need to learn to find their own center, they need to create a safe space of their own *separate from you*, and they need your help doing so. So if your kid wakes up from a bad dream, you should go to them. Even if they come to your room to fetch you, I want you to walk them back to their bed and do your hugging, consoling, or lying down with them there. Be sure to let them know that what they experienced came from their imagination and didn't actually happen, and do your best to ground your response in the familiar and the concrete. ("Deer can't fly." "Dinosaurs stopped existing a long time ago." "George Bush will be out of office very soon.") But once they've calmed down adequately, you need to separate. Remember, the goal here is to set up an appropriate and functional template for your child's future responses. Contrary to what you learned from Freddy Krueger, no child ever died from a nightmare: they're scary, but they're not the end of the world. Help them relax and move on. If you make it a big issue, you'll have a big issue on your hands.

NOSE PICKING

While a tissue is great when you have a runny or stuffy nose, you're a liar if you say that it trumps a finger for getting the hard clumpy stuff out of your nostrils. There's nothing like the satisfaction of plucking out a really big booger, except perhaps letting loose a pent-up burp or fart or taking a giant above-the-water-line dump. Propriety demands, however, that such activities be conducted in private. I think it's fine to let your kid dig around in their nose away from the prying eyes of the general public (you can decide if this includes you or not). Frankly, teaching them to self-pick is a hell of a lot less grody than having to scrounge around in there yourself. Just be sure to alert them as to where you believe nasal mining is acceptable and where it isn't—and in the not-okay places, teach them to hide their activities behind the social shroud of a Kleenex. Oh, and if they're going to go in unprotected, make sure they wash their hands before and after; hand-to-nose contact is one of the top means by which colds are transmitted.

ONANISM

Like most animals young children are natural pleasure seekers. And since one of the few objects to which they have unfettered access is their own body, it's only a matter of time before they discover the glories of what the ancients called self-love. *This is totally normal behavior* and should not be shut down. But unless you're a dog or a caged monkey, it's also a personal and private matter and should be relegated to appropriate times and places. It's up to you to let your kid know what you think these times and places are, but I would propose that you use a public/private boundary: it's not okay at the dinner table or during circle time, but it's fine in their bedroom or during nap at home. Or it's not okay at the doctor's office or on the subway, but it's fine while they're watching "train porn" in the living room (see Introduction).

SHYNESS

Being a good classroom teacher almost requires a performative nature, so it should come as no surprise that I'm an enormous ham. But being a good classroom teacher also requires that you learn how to connect with kids who have a temperament (see chapter 9) that differs from your own. This is often the root of a parent's issue with a shy kid: if the parent isn't shy themselves, they don't get what the big deal is about engaging with the world. But a slow-to-warm (shy) temperament is a real and inborn characteristic, and you have to be sensitive to it. At the same time it's not completely immutable, so don't back your child into a corner too early by constantly telling them, and everyone around them, "she's shy." While I believe that kids should learn to engage with the world, as with most things in early childhood, trying to force the issue will inevitably backfire. First off, no child *needs* to be social before around age three—kids are often not developmentally capable of the requisite ego release—so if you're in this boat, *stand down and give it time.* If your child is older than this, provide a slow start: large, unstructured groups (like the playground) are overwhelming for shy kids, so let them cling to you here while simultaneously arranging for smaller, more intimate social settings—one on one, in a comforting space of their own (like your home) with people they've met before. A quality preschool can often help a child overcome shyness by providing structured, regular, multifaceted, and cumulative access to the social world.

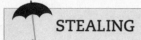

STEALING

Very young kids have an interesting take on material possessions, combining key aspects of communism and capitalism: their limited worldview literally fails to recognize private property rights, while their egocentric nature prevents them from understanding why they shouldn't have access to anything they see and desire. In addition, because they can neither ask for nor grant custody of any given object, most situations in which they take something that doesn't "belong" to them are by definition lacking in intentionality: they see, they like, they grab. So while you need to lay out the rules for them—ask before you take, return what you've been loaned—it also behooves you to teach them to be flexible: if they're not using every piece of their LEGO set, there's no reason why a peer shouldn't be able to borrow a brick or two. With slightly older kids, I'm all for biblical justice: if they steal once, cut off a finger; if they do it again, remove the hand. (Kidding!) But if you discover something in your child's possession that's clearly not theirs, don't presume the worst. Kids can be very generous; it could be an official gift or loan. So be sure to ask where it came from. Your child may not be able to answer clearly (see Lying, page 226), so you may have to do some gumshoeing of your own (asking the alleged owner's mom, quizzing the teacher, conducting unwarranted wiretaps). If you find that the object has been taken surreptitiously, don't waste your time with useless *why* questions (the answer's usually the same: *"Because I wanted it"*). Sternly remind your kid that they need to ask before taking things that don't belong to them, and involve them directly in returning it to its rightful owner. And don't panic. If you're calm and straightforward—and don't have a tremendous (and exciting) fit—it's unlikely that this will be their gateway to a life of crime.

WHINING

Discounting jokes about airport security; romantic comedies about Americans finding love abroad; and every single policy proposed, supported, or initiated by the Bush administration, there is little in the world more annoying than a whiny child. We all get tired and cranky sometimes, and because they're small and have less stamina, kids tend to get tired and cranky more frequently than we do. So a certain amount of whining is understandable and should be tolerated (but never enjoyed).

In actuality, most whiners are made, not born, so if you have one it's probably at least partly your fault. But it's never too late to change patterns or prevent new ones from taking root. Just do as I say. When your child whines—especially when the whine is attached to a question, request, or demand—simply remind them calmly to speak to you in a regular voice. If they continue to whine, repeat your admonishment and then ignore them until they abide. *Do not ever, under any circumstance, give in to whining* ("I want an ice cream, I want an ice cream"). If you do, your child will quickly come to believe this is an appropriate and effective means to get what they want, and I guarantee that you will have signed yourself, and anyone within earshot, up for a lifelong tasting in your child's extensive whine cellar. As difficult as it may be, firmly stating your position ("We're walking home and you need to walk on your own"), providing flat reminders as necessary ("I told you, we're walking home and I will not carry you"), and ignoring whining is really the only acceptable choice. You've learned to tune out the sound of your spouse/partner's voice; I know you can learn to add this to your repertoire of the inaudible.

Epilogue

I'VE PERSONALLY HAD a blast working on this book, and since my core goal is for you to have as much fun as a parent as I do as an uncle I hope your enjoyment factor approaches this on at least some fractional level. Remember, life with kids is supposed to be pleasurable. (Besides all that altruistic nonsense about continuing the glorious reign of the human species, isn't that why you had the little buggers in the first place?) So while I encourage you to take your job description seriously— particularly the *parenting* part of being a parent—don't take it all *too* seriously. Kids aren't inherently good or kind, but they are usually cute and hilarious. Now that you've read the instruction manual and learned how they work, see what you can do to dwell on that bit.

Like parenthood, Uncledom is for life. So know that I'll always be here for you. (In this book, that is. Do *not* try to find me.) In fact, I'm busy right now writing more Gay Uncle's Guides, and if this one sells well enough (hint, hint) I may even be given the opportunity to publish the others and share them with you. If not, the

Internet's a cheap and available platform so if you need a *GUG* fix you can always log on to www.askgayuncle.com. I can't promise that I'll be able to answer every letter you write, or every question you submit, but I vow to at least send a falsely personal autoreply message that thanks you for asking and shamelessly promotes whatever else I might be selling at the time.

Happy parenting!

Your Gay Uncle,
Brett

Acknowledgments

I WANT TO thank all the people who shared their parenting expertise with me and guided me on my path to writing this book, particularly Ian Chorao; Sylvia Sichel; Erica Heilman; Michele Clark; Ziyad Hopkins; Andrea Summers; Alison Shonkwiler; Saskia Grooms; Rob Young; Stacie Berk; Rob Eggers; Kirk Melnikoff; Paige; Andy; Gretchen; Anne; and Uncas McThenia, and my own parents, Barry Berk and Donna Barnett. I want to thank all my brilliant nieces and nephews, biological or otherwise, for making me an uncle: Malcolm, Sadie, Hannah, Sophie, Tessa, Whitley, Emma, Finley, Sarah, Leila, Nadia, Franklin, and Henry. I'm also indebted to the inspiring staff, students, and families from Chickpeas and Little Missionary's Day Nursery where I taught, and the folks from JKI, Relevant Research, Insight, and CMOM for keeping me in business while I wrote. I'm deeply and eternally grateful to my friend Colin Dickerman for helping usher this project into the world. And I couldn't have done it without the expert guidance of my agent, Daniel Greenberg, and my editor, Heather Jackson.

Of course, nothing in my life would be possible without the other Gay Uncle, Tal McThenia, who still claims that this whole thing was his idea.

Index

Index

Index

About the Author

BRETT BERK has worked in the field of early childhood education for more than twenty years, happily doing time as a tutor, a teacher, and a preschool director before moving out of the classroom to become a researcher and consultant. He now works with some of the biggest producers of toys, products, and media for young kids, including ABC, Cartoon Network, Disney Channel, General Mills, Hasbro, Hershey's, Hot Wheels, Kraft, Mattel, National Geographic, Nickelodeon, PBS, Scholastic, Sesame Workshop, and WGBH-Boston, as well as the New York City Board of Education, and the U.S. Department of Education.

Brett is also a published writer of short fiction. His stories have appeared in journals including *FICTION, Tin House, The Mississippi Review*, and *Other Voices* and have garnered numerous grants and awards. Since 2000, he has been on the faculty of the Writing Program at the New School University in New York City.

Brett holds a bachelor's degree in creative writing from Oberlin College in Oberlin, Ohio, and a master's degree in early childhood and elementary education from Hunter College of the City University of New York. He divides his time between New York City and a house in upstate New York. He and his partner of eighteen years have no children of their own (nor do they ever plan to have any), but they're extremely proud of their role as gay uncles.